**tifo**

/ˈtiːfəʊ /

*noun*

a choreographed display in which fans in a sports stadium raise a large banner together or simultaneously hold up signs that together form a large image.

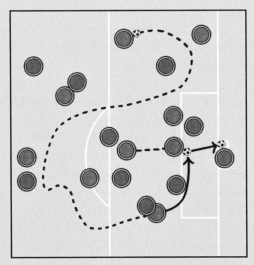

**FOOTBALL IS FOR EVERYONE. IT HAS SOMETHING FOR US ALL.**

**THIS BOOK IS A GUIDE TO ITS MANY LAYERS: A 52-CHAPTER MAP TO HELP YOU THROUGH THE GAME FROM ITS BEGINNINGS AND BASIC PRINCIPLES — THE OFFSIDE LAW, FORMATIONS, THE PITCH — THROUGH TO ITS MODERN TRENDS AND THE CHALLENGES IT FACES IN THE FUTURE.**

**EACH CHAPTER IS A GUIDELINE. WE'VE CALLED THEM RULES, BUT THEY'RE MORE LIKE *SUGGESTIONS*.**

Today, football is more complex on the pitch than it's ever been, and it has come to represent more away from it, too. Coaches preside over intricate tactical plans like architects, while powerful outside forces use the sport as a tool of soft power or for financial gain. And there's an awful lot in between, which can easily be undervalued. **We value it.**

While football will continue to grow and evolve, this book was written to give fans a foothold and enrich your enjoyment of the game. We want to start you off on your own journey. Towards what and with what aim? **That's up to you.**

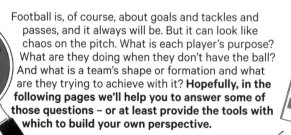

Football is, of course, about goals and tackles and passes, and it always will be. But it can look like chaos on the pitch. What is each player's purpose? What are they doing when they don't have the ball? And what is a team's shape or formation and what are they trying to achieve with it? **Hopefully, in the following pages we'll help you to answer some of those questions – or at least provide the tools with which to build your own perspective.**

'Pressing triggers', 'zonal marking', 'one-twos' and 'switching the play'; **we'll explain what these terms mean and where they came from.** We also attack a few myths, looking at why fouls aren't always bad, why playing with more defenders isn't always a defensive move, and why you shouldn't groan when your team takes a short corner.

## HOW SHOULD YOU WATCH FOOTBALL?

## WELL, REALLY ANY WAY YOU WANT TO. THINK OF THIS BOOK AS A PROSPECTUS FOR WHAT THE GAME OFFERS. A CATALOGUE OF NICHES, SO TO SPEAK, AND AN EXPLORATION OF ITS QUIRKS AND CONVENTIONS.

And those aren't confined to the pitch. We discuss the rise of data, and why statisticians are among the most valuable, unseen staff that many clubs employ. What are Expected Goals and Directors of Football? How does a throw-in coach make a difference? How do football clubs find players and make money?

**That's in here, too.**

The biggest question might be why football is played at all; we'll get right to the heart of that. Matches may be fought between teams of eleven, but – really – they're now often contests between billionaires and big corporations, sometimes governments and countries too. What does that mean? And is success measured in cups and titles any more, or influence and publicity instead?

So, we want to help you understand why a player moves left or right, why they're pushing up or staying back, why a team passes long or short, why they defend deep and which footballing methodology they're using as they try to score goals. **We want to give you a different lens through which to watch football, whether that's from a stadium seat or a sofa, and regardless of how many games you've watched before.**

We also want to make more sense of football's broader definition: as an industry, a cultural force, a political tool. We explore its balance sheets, its broadcasting contracts, its winter breaks and its transfer decisions. We look at the game's history, charting its evolution through a list of pioneers and legends from both footballing antiquity and the recent past – though where it's going might just be more important. Should we be worried about carbon footprints and rising sea levels? What type of organizations should be allowed to buy football clubs? And if there are some that shouldn't, how can they be stopped?

## IN TRUTH, THIS BOOK ISN'T JUST ABOUT WATCHING FOOTBALL, IT'S ABOUT PLAYING IT, TALKING ABOUT IT, THINKING ABOUT IT, AND EVEN COACHING IT.

## FOOTBALL IS WHATEVER YOU WANT IT TO BE. WE HOPE THIS BOOK HELPS YOU TO DECIDE WHAT THAT IS.

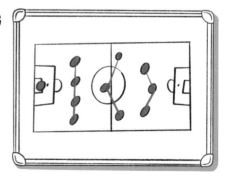

# HOW TO WATCH FOOTBALL

**Fifty-two rules for understanding the beautiful game, on and off the pitch**

# 1

# DON'T WATCH THE BALL

Redefine your understanding
of *what and where* the action is

**IN AN AVERAGE FOOTBALL GAME, AN AVERAGE FOOTBALL PLAYER WILL GET 4.6% OF THE TOTAL TOUCHES OF THE BALL. THAT EQUATES TO ABOUT SIXTY TOUCHES PER GAME IN A RECENT PREMIER LEAGUE SEASON. IT FOLLOWS THAT, FOR CLOSE TO 86 MINUTES OF THE GAME, MOST PLAYERS ARE WITHOUT THE BALL.**

As football fans, we're taught to follow the action; to watch the ball and the player who possesses it. It's the obvious and most entertaining choice. But the ball and the possessor are just the tip of the iceberg.

This is because for the 86 minutes that your average player is not in possession of the ball, they aren't just standing still. They are moving, pressing, marking and repositioning themselves. In other words, affecting the game. It is in these moments that football mostly happens, and yet as viewers we miss almost all of it.

Maybe no player better illustrates this than Xavi Hernández, Barcelona's great playmaker. Xavi is – understandably – remembered for his ability to distribute the ball, and yet it was often his ability to receive it, to find space and make himself available for teammates to pass to that really enabled him to orchestrate games.

In a career of profound influence, Xavi's best performance might have been in the 2011 Champions League final, against Manchester United at Wembley. **Of the 922 touches Barcelona had that night, Xavi accounted for 156 of them – an extraordinary level of involvement: 17% of his side's total and 11% of the game's.**

Those who just watched Xavi whenever he had the ball would have seen some beautiful and game-changing moments. But those who watched him for the full 90 minutes would have witnessed the real breadth of his authority – how he moved into space to make himself available to receive passes, how he dropped into position to cover defensively, and how he was continuously scanning the play and plotting where his next pass would go, even before he was given the ball.

## IF HE HAD 156 TOUCHES, IT'S BECAUSE HE MADE HIMSELF AVAILABLE 156 TIMES.

# DO WATCH THE LINES

## How pitch markings came to define football

**BACK IN 1863, A FOOTBALL PITCH WAS A BLANK CANVAS. THERE WERE NO MARKINGS TO SPEAK OF. THERE WERE GOALPOSTS, ALBEIT WITHOUT CROSSBARS, AND FLAGS THAT MARKED OUT THE CORNERS, BUT THE PITCH BORE LITTLE RESEMBLANCE TO WHAT IT WOULD BECOME.**

Its metamorphosis wouldn't begin until 1891, when goallines and touchlines around the perimeter were added, and the centre circle was introduced. A goalkeeper's area became part of the game too, although in the form of two half circles originating at each goalline.

The precursor to the penalty spot was also introduced though, again, not in a recognizable way. The original penalty spot was actually a line twelve yards from the goalline, which stretched right the way across the breadth of the pitch.

**IT WOULDN'T BE UNTIL 1902 THAT THE MODERN PITCH REALLY TOOK SHAPE.**

The penalty line finally became a spot. The penalty area took on its rectangular form. The halfway line was added, too, cutting through the centre circle at a point equidistant from each goal.

**AND THERE HAS ONLY BEEN ONE MORE CHANGE: THE PENALTY-AREA ARC, WHICH WAS INTRODUCED IN 1937.**

The D, as it's better known, is an iconic part of a football pitch's visual identity, and it has a very simple purpose. It's there to prevent encroachment when a penalty is being taken.

When a penalty is taken, every player apart from the taker must be outside the penalty area and at least ten yards away from the ball. The problem, prior to the D's introduction, was that it was very difficult for referees to judge any encroachment. **The D changed that.**

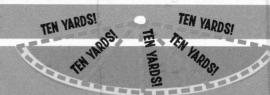

**EVERY POINT ON THE ARC IS EXACTLY TEN YARDS AWAY FROM THE PENALTY SPOT, PROVIDING AN INVALUABLE TOOL FOR OFFICIALS, AND COMPLETING THE PENALTY AREA AS IT LOOKS TODAY.**

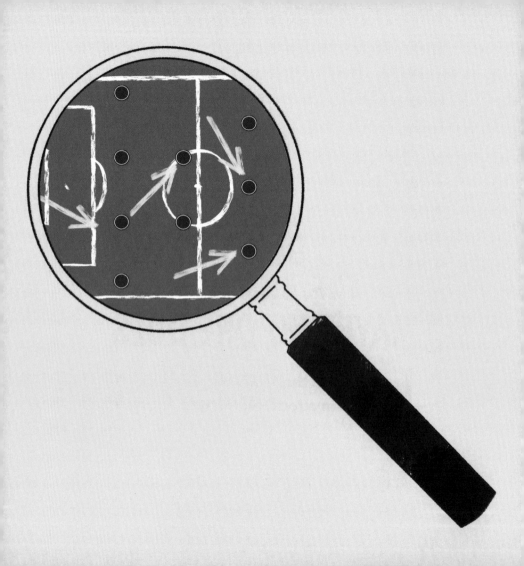

# IF YOU DON'T KNOW THE ANSWER, MAYBE NO ONE DOES

## Why are there eleven players in a football team?

**1.** People think of football as an English game, but it has diverse roots. Forms of the game were played by the Chinese in around **AD 200,** and the Aztecs developed a similar sport, too. In Italy, the game's ancestor is Calcio Fiorentino, a brutal sport originating in the Middle Ages, which to the modern eye looks closer to mixed martial arts, religious ceremony and rugby than to modern football.

**2.** In England, football dates from the eighth century. The aim of medieval 'mob' football was to transport an inflated pig's bladder from one end of a village to another by any means necessary. Injuries were common, deaths weren't unusual, and teams were often hundreds strong. It was chaos.

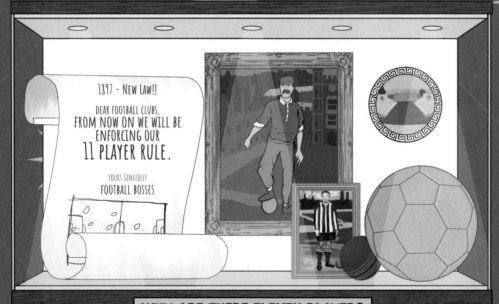

1897 - NEW LAW!!

DEAR FOOTBALL CLUBS,
FROM NOW ON WE WILL BE
ENFORCING OUR
11 PLAYER RULE.

YOURS SINCERELY
FOOTBALL BOSSES

## WHY ARE THERE ELEVEN PLAYERS IN A FOOTBALL TEAM?
*Well, nobody is quite sure.*

**3.** Medieval football is largely a thing of the past, though some forms do still exist, like the Atherstone Ball Game, which is played in the town of Atherstone, in Warwickshire, every Shrove Tuesday, between teams of indeterminate size. But it's a long way from the eleven-a-side game that we know today.

**4.** The journey from mob football to the modern game involved a few English public schools and plenty of compromise. The first laws – the Sheffield Rules – were published in 1858. The newly formed Football Association published its own version in 1863 and, although those rules became universal in 1877 (the same year that tripping and hacking were outlawed and the goal-kick was introduced), there was no mention of team size – anywhere.

Twenty years later, the International Football Association Board, which was formed to reconcile the differences in rules between the English, Welsh, Scottish and Irish Football Associations, and which is still the game's lawmaker to this day, wrote eleven players into the rules as one of its standardizing amendments.

But that was hardly revolutionary; eleven players on each side had actually been the convention for the past few decades. So, how did that happen?

It might just have been trial and error. Some think that, following the introduction of a goalkeeper in 1871, eleven players might have gradually become a norm, as an ideal number for the various roles on the pitch or the amount of space that needed filling.

Another theory is attractive and very simple. Many British football clubs trace their origins back to cricket, with the sport serving as a means for cricketers to stay fit through the winter months. So maybe the eleven players of a cricket team naturally became eleven footballers – out of convenience, perhaps?

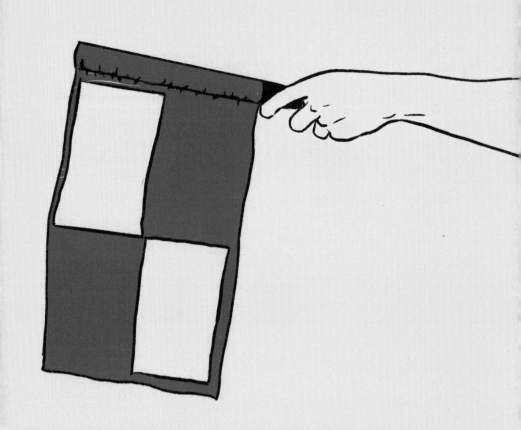

# 4

# MOST RULES ARE THERE FOR A REASON

## The evolution of the offside rule

FROM THEIR INTRODUCTION, MOST OF FOOTBALL'S LAWS WERE TWEAKED AND REFINED TO IMPROVE THE GAME. THE OFFSIDE RULE IS NO DIFFERENT. TODAY, THE DEFINITION OF OFFSIDE IS SIMPLE: AT THE MOMENT AT WHICH A PASS IS PLAYED, AN ATTACKING PLAYER IN THE OPPOSITION'S HALF MUST EITHER BE BEHIND OR LEVEL WITH THE BALL, OR OTHERWISE HAVE TWO OPPOSING PLAYERS BETWEEN THEM AND THE GOAL THAT THEY'RE ATTACKING.

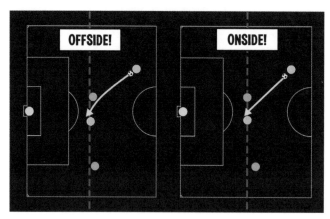

It's a finely balanced rule that seems fair to both the attacking and the defending players. That hasn't always been the case, though. In fact, while almost untouched now for nearly a century, the offside laws have undergone many revisions.

In the original Football Association rulebook, a player was offside if they were in front of the ball when it was kicked. No ifs, buts or maybes; it didn't even matter whether or not that player was receiving a pass.

That didn't really encourage a passing game or very many goals. The intention had been to prevent goal-hanging (loitering around the opposition's goal), but the consequence was to create a low-scoring, dour spectacle. So, in **1866,** the first revision was introduced, making it a rule that a player would be onside either if they were behind the ball when it was kicked or if there were three opposition players between them and the goal they were attacking. One of those players was typically the goalkeeper, but it still encouraged very cautious football.

In **1903,** the idea of 'interfering with play' was introduced, which created a grey area in the laws that still exists to this day. It meant that if a player wasn't involved in, or affecting, the play, then there would be no offside.

In **1925,** again in pursuit of a more attacking game, the number of defenders needed between an attacking player and the goal was reduced from three to two, and that was very much the magic formula; from that moment, the offside law has remained relatively unchanged.

Slight tweaks have been made, however. After the **1990 World Cup,** for instance, it was determined that players could be level with defenders and remain onside. That was another measure to favour the attacking team.

Then, **at the beginning of the twenty-first century,** it was decreed that a player could only be offside if a part of their body with which a goal could be scored had crossed the offside line.

And so it has remained. The only innovations relating to offside since have concerned how it's adjudicated and the impact of the Video Assistant Referee (VAR), which was introduced to provide technical oversight over refereeing decisions. Maybe that'll inspire a future tweak? The more technology has allowed officials to be precise, the more pedantic offside decisions have become – and perhaps that's counter to the spirit of the game?

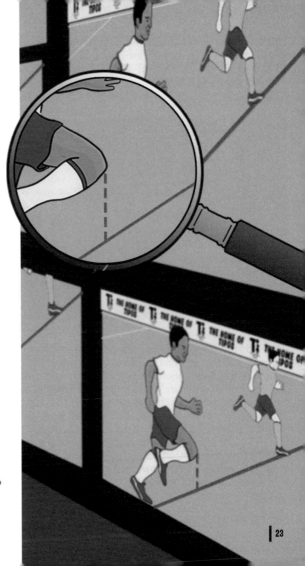

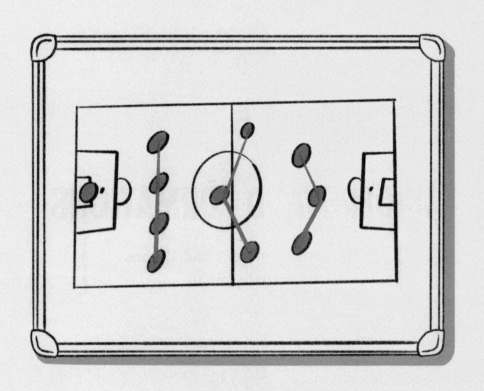

# 5

# UNDERSTAND FORMATIONS

What the numbers and shapes
actually mean

**A FORMATION IS A JIGSAW: IT ONLY MAKES SENSE IF THE INDIVIDUAL PIECES FIT TOGETHER AND ARE ASSEMBLED CORRECTLY. A COACH HAS TO FIND A FORMATION THAT SUITS THE ABILITIES OF THE PLAYERS AVAILABLE, BUT ALSO THWARTS THE THREATS AND CHALLENGES PRESENTED BY THE OPPOSITION.**

**EVERY FORMATION IS A COMPROMISE OF STRENGTHS AND WEAKNESSES.**

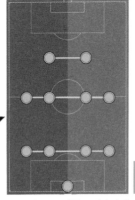

TRADITIONAL
4-4-2
VS
3-5-2

TRADITIONAL
4-4-2

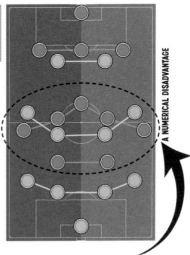

A NUMERICAL DISADVANTAGE

For instance, the traditional 4-4-2, with its four defenders, four midfielders and two forwards, is **evenly spaced, secure and has a simplicity** that makes it easy for most players to master; but it has its flaws. The positions are **rigid,** and that's a factor exploited by many modern managers who prefer a three-player central midfield, in the form either of a 3-5-2 or a 4-3-3.

Facing those teams, a side in a 4-4-2 formation, with two central midfielders and a pair of wingers each side, will often find itself at **a numerical disadvantage** in the middle of the pitch and face difficulty in retaining and advancing possession.

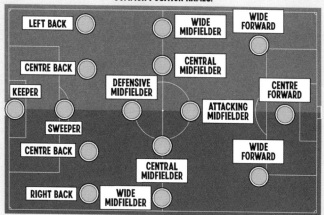

**COMMON POSITION NAMES:**

LEFT BACK
CENTRE BACK
KEEPER
SWEEPER
CENTRE BACK
RIGHT BACK
WIDE MIDFIELDER
DEFENSIVE MIDFIELDER
CENTRAL MIDFIELDER
WIDE MIDFIELDER
ATTACKING MIDFIELDER
CENTRAL MIDFIELDER
WIDE FORWARD
CENTRE FORWARD
WIDE FORWARD

Equally, though, despite the advantages of a system like 3-5-2, in which an extra midfield player is available, there will always be an issue to overcome somewhere else. Playing one defender fewer means allowing the opposition more space up front; it also requires a centre forward of unusual size and ability, who can play with only wingers for support rather than an actual partner, or second forward.

**There's no right answer; every team comprises different players with unique strengths and weaknesses, and there's no such thing as a system that works equally well for everyone.** Moreover, because of the way football evolves and player 'types' are always falling in and out of fashion, what works today might not be quite as optimal in ten years' time.

At the dawn of the Premier League, for instance, back in the 1990s, almost every team in the top-flight played 4-4-2 with two strikers in attack, usually of contrasting and complementary abilities. Within a decade, the trend had moved towards 4-3-3, with those two strikers being replaced by one centre forward, and the wingers from the 4-4-2 being recast as wide forwards either side of that one player.

**FORMATIONS ARE A RESPONSE – TO STRENGTHS, TO WEAKNESSES, AND TO THE FOOTBALL FASHIONS OF THE DAY.**

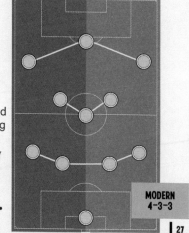

MODERN 4-3-3

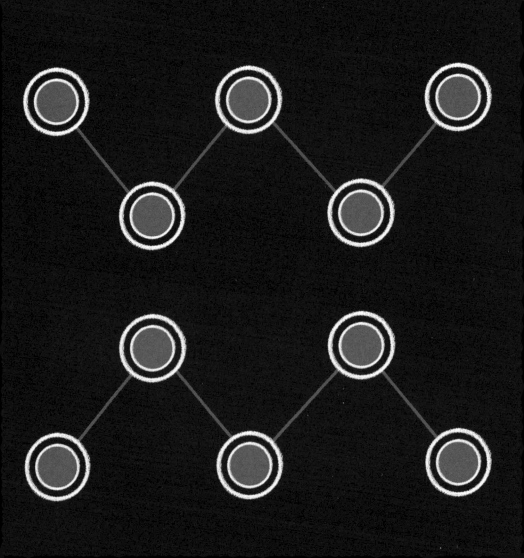

# 6

# KNOW YOUR INFLUENCES:
## HERBERT CHAPMAN
### (1878–1934)

The original
innovator

**HERBERT CHAPMAN WASN'T SO MUCH AN INFLUENCE ON FOOTBALL AS ONE OF ITS PIONEERS. WHILE A MANAGER, CHAPMAN WON THE FIRST DIVISION FOUR TIMES – TWICE WITH HUDDERSFIELD AND TWICE WITH ARSENAL – AND HE LED BOTH CLUBS TO WIN THE FA CUP.**

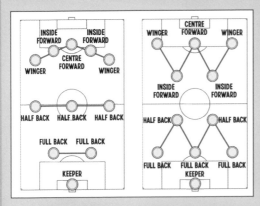

COMMON FORMATION BEFORE THE RULE CHANGE (2-3-5)

THE NEW W-M FORMATION

**When the offside rule changed in 1925,** it allowed a forward to be played onside by two defenders instead of three, encouraging teams to play a more attacking game and to commit greater numbers forward. Chapman's W-M (or 3-2-2-3) formation was a response to that. It converted the centre half in its predecessor, the 2-3-5, into a centre back at the heart of a back three – thus providing greater defensive protection.

**It was the basis of Chapman's successful Arsenal sides of the early 1930s and their hugely effective style of play.** During an era in which there was little tactical cohesion between players, and when the tendency was to get the ball forward with long, direct kicks up the pitch, Chapman favoured a snappier game, with short passes, careful build-up, and quick, dynamic wingers.

He was the author of all sorts of other changes, too, and the source of a raft of different ideas, many of which remain in the game today. Arsenal's shirts have white sleeves, for instance, because he thought it would make it easier for his players to spot their teammates. It was his idea that football shirts should be numbered, that floodlights should be installed at Highbury, and that tactics could be used to explain players' roles in team meetings. Even the idea of discussing tactics at all was new, as was the idea in England that a system could win games.

But his influence extended well beyond the chalkboard. He was behind London's Gillespie Road tube station being renamed 'Arsenal', and he was part of the club's decision to drop its 'the' prefix so that it would begin each season atop of the league table in alphabetical order.

HE ALSO REMADE HIS OWN ROLE. HIS PEERS, THE OTHER COACHES OF THE TIME, WERE 'TRAINERS' REALLY, TASKED WITH PICKING THE TEAM AND LITTLE ELSE.

**Chapman broke that mould.**

He was involved in scouting and reserve teams, long before that was typical, and he created training schedules, too. He was involved in almost everything – essentially, he defined the contemporary football manager decades before the concept existed. He exerted influence of a breadth that wouldn't become normal until many years after his untimely death in 1934.

---

### TIFO EXPLAINS: THE FOOTBALL LEAGUE

The current league system in England is misleading. There are four professional divisions, of which the Premier League is the highest. Below that, in order, are the EFL (English Football League) Championship, the EFL League One and the EFL League Two. That's a fairly modern change, with the Premier League coming into being only in 1992. Before that, from its 1888 creation onwards, the ordering was simpler, with the First Division the highest, the Second Division below it and so on.

# 7

# LEARN TO SPOT THE DIFFERENCE

## Zonal marking vs player marking

When a football team is defending, they have two main ways to stop an opponent scoring goals. One is to disrupt the opponents' play directly by putting pressure on the player. The other way is to protect space and stop the opponent from advancing the ball into areas from where they could score. These two different approaches have led to two different types of defensive system: player marking (commonly known as man marking) and zonal marking.

## PLAYER MARKING

In a player-marking system, a team will look to **orientate itself defensively by marking – or getting close to – opposition players:**

The **benefits** of player marking are that it offers an effective way of covering the opposition. Player-to-player pressure makes it hard for an opponent to construct moves, and there is clarity for the defending team as to what each individual's responsibility is.

But it has its **downsides:** first and foremost, it requires a huge amount of physical exertion to follow an opponent around a pitch for 90 minutes. On top of that, the fact that defending players have to track opponents can mean that the opposition can pull the defending team's structure apart, creating space for other players to exploit.

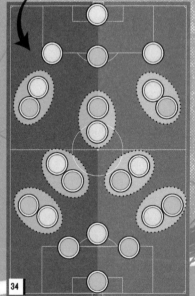

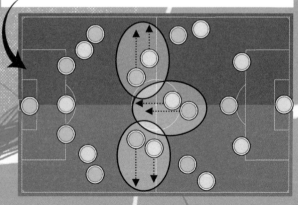

# ZONAL MARKING

For these reasons, most teams will use a **zonal-marking defensive system.** Instead of marking players, the defending team are now covering 'zones' on the pitch:

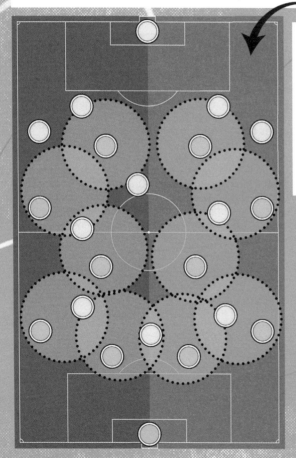

Defending the areas that they're responsible for prevents players from being dragged out of position with the same ease as in a player-marking system.

But this system has its **downsides,** too. Oppositions can cause problems by overloading or switching zones, creating confusion for the defending team as to who is responsible for whom.

AS WITH FORMATIONS, THERE IS NO PERFECT DEFENSIVE MARKING SYSTEM. EACH TEAM TAILORS THEIR APPROACH AROUND WHO THEY HAVE AVAILABLE AND WHAT KIND OF OPPOSITION THEY'RE FACING. SOMETIMES, THE ANSWER IS EVEN A COMBINATION OF THE TWO: PLAYER MARKING A PARTICULARLY DANGEROUS PLAYER, WHILE ADOPTING A MORE ZONAL STRATEGY ACROSS THE REST OF THE PITCH.

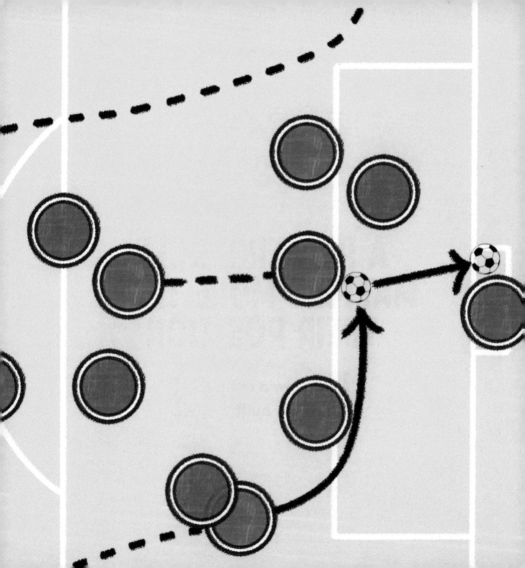

# 8

# A PLAYER'S ROLE MATTERS MORE THAN THEIR POSITION

## How a team is built

**Formations. The bedrock of modern football. The humble 4-4-2. The fashionable 3-4-3.**

These numbers represent **positions,** and we give these positions names that indicate where each player probably spends most of their time on the pitch, like **'centre back'** or **'defensive midfielder',** or sometimes what their main job is, like **'striker'.**

**But, today, these labels are too simplistic.** Compare three different full backs, each operating in a back-four defence. One might **stay deep,** allowing the opposite full back to push high and creating a back-three shape. One might **push very high in attack,** trying to overlap and beat their opposite number to whip in crosses. And one might **tuck into central midfield.**

Or, put simply: Arsenal's Takehiro Tomiyasu, Aston Villa's Matty Cash, and Liverpool's Trent Alexander-Arnold, for example. They're all **'full backs',** but their roles are very different.

Positions create expectations for someone watching football, but the complexity and tactical nuances of the modern game mean that they are just a starting point. **No two central midfielders do exactly the same job,** even if they mostly stay in the same part of the pitch. One might **pass expressively and take risks with the ball to create chances;** another may just **tackle, win the ball back, and play simple, short passes** to the closest teammate.

## FULL BACKS
### BUY 3 GET 1 FREE!

MODERN FULL BACKS NEW PACK!

DIFFERENT DEFENCE STYLES!

'STAYS DEEP' STYLE!

BUY 3 GET ONE FREE

'TUCKS IN' STYLE!

'PUSHES HIGH' STYLE!

**WHEN WE THINK ABOUT PLAYERS, THEN, WE SHOULD BE THINKING ABOUT ROLES.**

**WHAT DOES THIS PLAYER ACTUALLY DO FOR THEIR TEAM?**

**ARE THEY THE CREATIVE HUB, DESPITE BEING A FULL BACK?**

**DOES THIS STRIKER LURK ON THE SHOULDER TO RUN IN BEHIND, OR DROP DEEP TO ORCHESTRATE ATTACKING MOVES FOR QUICK WIDE ATTACKERS?**

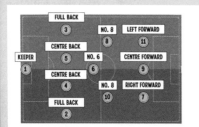

**POSITIONS IN A 4-3-3**

FULL BACK
(3)

NO. 8
(8)

LEFT FORWARD
(11)

CENTRE BACK
(5)

NO. 6
(6)

KEEPER
(1)

CENTRE FORWARD
(9)

CENTRE BACK
(4)

NO. 8
(10)

RIGHT FORWARD
(7)

FULL BACK
(2)

Rather than fix our expectations of what a player should be doing, it would be better to focus on what they actually *are* doing and how that works within the team. **Forget positions; look at roles.**

# DON'T RUN IN TRAINING

**The rise of
tactical periodization**

## WELL, DON'T RUN AIMLESSLY.

A decade or two ago, most accounts of pre-season training or general conditioning included long, exhausting runs. And this was accepted as good practice.

Go back a century, and you'll find that running was often the only preparation done ahead of matches. Starve a player of the ball during the week, and they were more likely to want it at the weekend – or so went the wisdom of the day. But, now, the idea that fitness and football are separate and cannot be worked on simultaneously has been disproven.

Enter **tactical periodization** (or a small element of it, at least): the footballing pedagogy famously embraced by the likes of **José Mourinho and André Villas-Boas.**

| WEDS | THURS | FRI | SAT | SUN |
|------|-------|-----|-----|-----|
|  |  |  | MATCH DAY | REST DAY |
| 4-4-2 | RIGHT SIDE OF TEAM | TACTICAL BRIEFING |  |  |
| PRESSING | STRIKER RUNS |  |  |  |
| ...DURANCE | SPEED | VERTICAL PRESSING |  |  |

### TIFO EXPLAINS: TACTICAL PERIODIZATION

Tactical periodization roots the training framework in tactics, which is seen as the game's governing dynamic. Fitness, technique, even psychology, are therefore all trained within that context.

Sessions are planned around a rolling schedule that builds up towards games and takes the season's ebb and flow into account, so that, while every discipline is covered, the order and intensity of sessions are devised to fit the actual footballing calendar, and to guard against fatigue.

Building on the tenets
of the Portuguese academic Vitor Frade,
Mourinho trains his players in scenarios
designed to mimic phases of the game: *attacking,
defending, transition from attacking to defending, and
transition from defending to attacking.*

Tactical periodization is
obviously much more complicated
than just training with the ball at your feet,
but that's a good place to start. Creating drills that mimic phases of
the game ensures that running occurs within a proper, useful context
and in a way that more accurately targets particular muscles, for
example, and more efficiently trains certain disciplines.

After all, while a 90-minute jog might be good preparation for
an Olympic track athlete, running in a football match is very
different. Players stop, start and change speeds and
directions continuously, while performing a
combination of tactical and
technical tasks.

SO, DO RUN IN TRAINING, BUT DON'T RUN THE WRONG WAY.

# 10

# KNOW YOUR INFLUENCES:
## JIMMY HOGAN
### (1882–1974)

The nomad
coach

## JIMMY HOGAN IS PROBABLY THE MOST INFLUENTIAL ENGLISH FOOTBALL COACH IN HISTORY, BUT HIS ACHIEVEMENTS ARE TOO OFTEN FORGOTTEN.

Born in Lancashire in 1882, Hogan played professionally, but his exploits in Europe as a coach, with the Austrian, Swiss and Hungarian national teams, and MTK Budapest at club level, are what mark him out as such a pioneering figure.

Hogan was an early exponent of **the Combination Game,** a style of football based on passing and movement rather than direct, long kicking and physicality. But he quickly evolved this to an even more extreme style of passing and positional rotation that has echoes in **Total Football.** Hogan emphasized rigorous physical preparation but also, unusually, gave a lot of training time to technical and tactical preparation. Hogan felt that players should be positionally versatile, able to fill different roles at different times and to react instinctively to the changing positions of their teammates.

Pass and move – a player passing a ball, then moving into space after they've released it.

Hogan coached **MTK Budapest to ten consecutive Hungarian league titles in the 1920s,** introducing concepts such as **pass-and-move** and **positional rotation.** He also coached in the Netherlands, Switzerland and France, but his influence is most clearly seen with the great Austrian national team of the 1930s, where he worked closely alongside the head coach Hugo Meisl, and with **Hungary's Mighty Magyars of the 1950s.**

AFTER HUNGARY'S FAMOUS 6–3 WIN AT WEMBLEY IN 1953, A RESULT THAT SHOOK FOOTBALL'S ESTABLISHMENT TO ITS CORE, THEIR COACH GUSZTÁV SEBES SAID,

'WE PLAYED FOOTBALL AS JIMMY HOGAN TAUGHT US. WHEN OUR FOOTBALL HISTORY IS TOLD, HIS NAME SHOULD BE WRITTEN IN GOLD LETTERS.'

47

# 11

# CORNERS ARE LESS EFFECTIVE THAN YOU THINK

A story of expectations vs success rate

IT'S THE LAST MINUTE OF A GAME. WITH A GOAL TO FIND, A TEAM FORCES A CORNER. THE FANS RISE TO THEIR FEET; THE STADIUM RUMBLES WITH THE ANTICIPATION OF ONE LAST CHANCE.

# BUT IS IT REALLY
# A CHANCE?

## IF IT IS, IT'S NOT A VERY BIG ONE.

Since 2010, only 3% of the corners taken in Europe's top five leagues have resulted in a goal. For goals scored directly from corners (that is, shots taken with the very next touch), it's only between 1 and 2%.

**TIFO TALKS: NUMBERS**

3%

'NOT VERY MANY'

GOALS SCORED FROM CORNERS TAKEN IN EUROPE'S TOP FIVE LEAGUES (SINCE 2010)

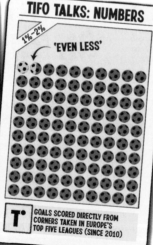

**TIFO TALKS: NUMBERS**

1%-2%

'EVEN LESS'

GOALS SCORED DIRECTLY FROM CORNERS TAKEN IN EUROPE'S TOP FIVE LEAGUES (SINCE 2010)

A bit of context tells us that only 7% of corners lead even to shots on goal, let alone actual goals, so at least we know that the likelihood of a goal from a shot on target following a corner is relatively high.

**The problem starts earlier.** And that might be because four out of every ten corners taken fail to beat the first defender.

## SO, WHY ARE FOOTBALL PLAYERS SO BAD AT CORNERS?

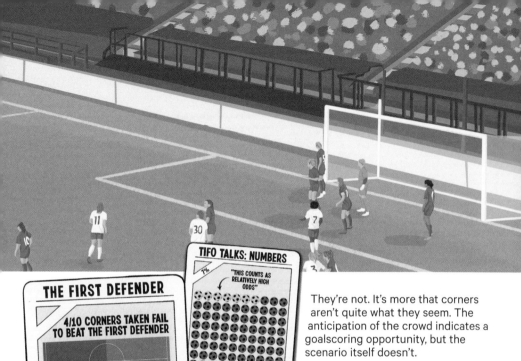

## THE FIRST DEFENDER

### 4/10 CORNERS TAKEN FAIL TO BEAT THE FIRST DEFENDER

IN THIS SCENARIO, NO. 2 IS THE FIRST DEFENDER

**T°** THE FIRST DEFENDER

All data by Stats Perform

### TIFO TALKS: NUMBERS

2% "THIS COUNTS AS RELATIVELY HIGH ODDS"

**T°** SHOTS TAKEN ON GOAL FROM CORNERS TAKEN IN EUROPE'S TOP-FIVE LEAGUES (SINCE 2010)

They're not. It's more that corners aren't quite what they seem. The anticipation of the crowd indicates a goalscoring opportunity, but the scenario itself doesn't.

A corner is a cross delivered from the touchline, at an unfavourable angle and into a crowded penalty area where defenders generally outnumber attackers. And where a goalkeeper is likely to catch or punch away a ball arriving within the six-yard box (the smaller rectangle inside the penalty area).

For a goal to be scored from a corner, several difficult things need to go right concurrently. **Which is why, roughly 98 times out of 100, a corner leaves the attacking team's fans disappointed.**

## 12

# SHORT CORNERS ARE ACTUALLY GOOD

### A *different* story of expectations vs success rate

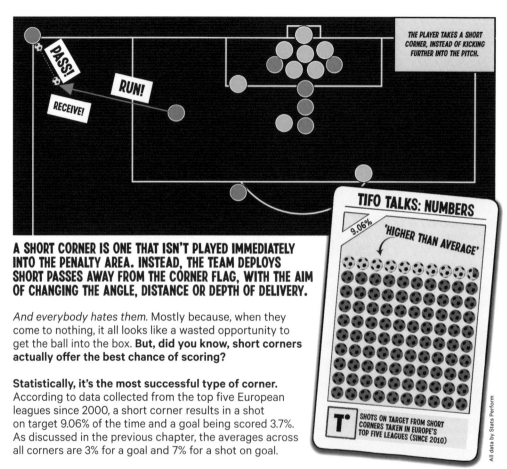

THE PLAYER TAKES A SHORT CORNER, INSTEAD OF KICKING FURTHER INTO THE PITCH.

PASS!

RUN!

RECEIVE!

## TIFO TALKS: NUMBERS

9.06%

'HIGHER THAN AVERAGE'

T° SHOTS ON TARGET FROM SHORT CORNERS TAKEN IN EUROPE'S TOP FIVE LEAGUES (SINCE 2010)

All data by Stats Perform

## A SHORT CORNER IS ONE THAT ISN'T PLAYED IMMEDIATELY INTO THE PENALTY AREA. INSTEAD, THE TEAM DEPLOYS SHORT PASSES AWAY FROM THE CORNER FLAG, WITH THE AIM OF CHANGING THE ANGLE, DISTANCE OR DEPTH OF DELIVERY.

*And everybody hates them.* Mostly because, when they come to nothing, it all looks like a wasted opportunity to get the ball into the box. **But, did you know, short corners actually offer the best chance of scoring?**

**Statistically, it's the most successful type of corner.** According to data collected from the top five European leagues since 2000, a short corner results in a shot on target 9.06% of the time and a goal being scored 3.7%. As discussed in the previous chapter, the averages across all corners are 3% for a goal and 7% for a shot on goal.

**By some distance, the short corner is the best option. Why?**

Most obviously because it improves the angle of delivery. **(A)** Instead of a flat cross, a well-worked routine can play the crosser into a more dangerous position and, under the right circumstances, an area far closer to goal.

Also, because the natural response to a short corner is for defenders to put pressure on the ball, taking one removes another body from the penalty area – sometimes more than one. **(B)**

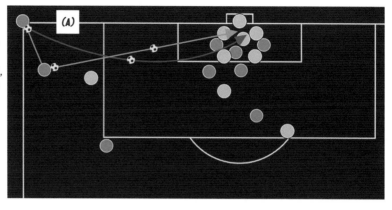

While most attacking sides use two players for a short corner, some use three. Either way, the result – with good execution – is generally a numerical mismatch that creates an overlap, more space and, as a consequence, the removal of some of the difficulties that corner-takers face.

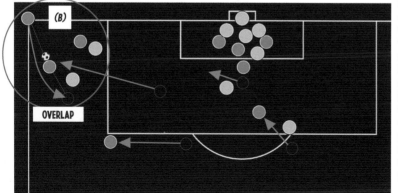

Depending on how adventurous a team is, that might fashion a shooting opportunity before the ball even enters the box, thereby turning a corner, with its illusory promise, into something closer to an attacking free kick.

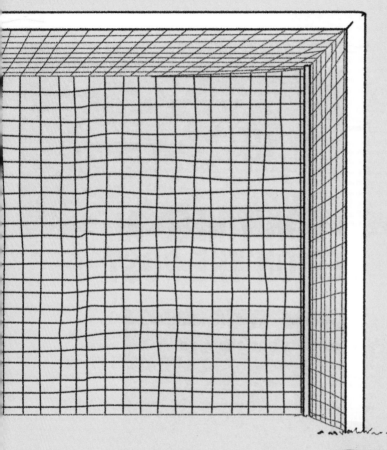

# 13

# YOU DON'T NEED A PLAYER ON THE POST

| How and why defending corners has changed |

# A CORNER IS TAKEN AND AN ATTACKER RISES TO MEET THE CROSS AND HEADS TOWARDS GOAL.

## THE GOALKEEPER, UNABLE TO REACT IN TIME TO MAKE A SAVE, WATCHES IN DESPAIR AS THE BALL HITS THE POST AND GOES IN.

The response in this situation is for fans, pundits and commentators to complain about the lack of defenders on the posts. **It's ancient football lore:** when defending a corner, a team should have one player guarding the near post and one protecting the back post.

**BUT HOW USEFUL IS THAT? THERE ARE, IN FACT, SEVERAL REASONS WHY YOU DON'T NEED PLAYERS ON THE POST AT ALL.**

The first is **marking.** It's more useful to have players who can contest the ball. Deploying one or two players to guard a space where the ball may or may not go, as opposed to one actually containing an opposition player, is just a waste.

This is partly because of the second issue, **the offside rule.** It's essentially impossible to be offside directly from a corner, but the phase of play often continues. While a defender on the post can push up into the box once the ball is cleared, sometimes they're slow to do that or hesitant in leaving their position.

By staying back, these defenders play everyone onside, and that means any attacker who can push past the main body of markers is free in a scoring position. This is very dangerous, especially because, while few goals are scored directly from a corner, follow-ups can be fruitful attacking opportunities once some defensive structure has broken down.

# 14

# KNOW YOUR INFLUENCES:
## THE MIGHTY MAGYARS
## (1950s)

**When Hungary ruled the world**

# THE HUNGARY TEAM OF THE 1950S HAS A GENUINE CLAIM TO BE THE BEST INTERNATIONAL SIDE EVER.

In 1953, Hungary were Olympic champions and on a 24-game unbeaten streak. They travelled to Wembley to play England, who were viewed – in England, at least – as football's finest exponents. And not without cause: England had only been beaten once on home turf, and the Football Association felt that their national side was the fittest and most technical in the world, despite not having proven themselves on the international stage..

**Hungary won 6–3.** As a result, England were forced to overhaul their tactics, preparation and approach.

The so-called **'Game of the Century'** highlighted just how far ahead Hungary were, thanks to their coach, **Gusztáv Sebes**.

Sebes wanted each of his players to be able to *inhabit any role or position required* in a match situation. He emphasized picking national teams based on a strong core of players who worked together at clubs, rather than just the best individuals. He insisted on his players' physical fitness, and also developed a **3-2-3-2 formation**. This saw the use of a **'false 9'**, or deeper central striker, **Nándor Hidegkuti**, who played much further from goal than usual, with Ferenc Puskás and Sándor Kocsis ahead of him and able to drift wide or cut infield at

will. The Hungarians' fluidity so bewildered the English players – who were used to man marking by shirt numbers – that it pulled their defence totally out of shape. This tactic would echo through to the Dutch concept of Total Football, and its influence can still be felt today.

The seeds of Hungary's enormous success in this period, during which they lost only one match **(the World Cup final against West Germany in 1954),** had been sown during the interwar years, in the coffee houses of the Danube region. Football was an almost scholarly pursuit: art critics and academics rubbed shoulders with coaches and players to discuss the game at places like the Ring Café in Vienna. Their ideas – about the value of short passing and co-ordinated, planned movement – were antithetical to football at the time, but after the war they proliferated through central Europe and reached their apogee in Hungary. The country was suffering under an oppressive Soviet regime, and Sebes' team became a source of national pride and a harmonious expression of individual talent working well within a system at odds with the dogmatic, authoritarian tone of the country at the time.

## TIFO EXPLAINS: THE FALSE 9

A false 9 is a forward who typically plays deeper than a traditional no. 9. Instead of playing as high up the pitch as possible, they will generally drop deeper, further away from the penalty area and into positions where they can receive and play passes and help develop moves.

# 15

# EXPECT MORE FROM THROW-INS

The story of an
under-utilized set piece

**IN THE 2020–21 PREMIER LEAGUE SEASON, TEAMS TOOK ON AVERAGE 19.6 THROW-INS PER GAME. OF THESE, 6.7 PER GAME WERE IN THE ATTACKING THIRD.**

**That's almost seven chances per game to do something clever and interesting,** and yet teams so rarely seem to, often simply electing to work the ball backwards or throw it up the line to be contested in the air.

Sport is all about '**marginal gains'**, a phrase popularized in cycling. It means finding and, crucially, adding up lots of little areas of improvement that equal an advantage over otherwise similarly strong opponents.

Some teams have spotted the marginal gains that throw-ins can offer. **Brentford,** for example, leaning on the lessons of their Danish sister club **FC Midtjylland,** try to capitalize on throw-ins by sending them deep into the opposition box with diverse off-the-ball movement from runners that forces defenders to react.

TIFO TALKS: NUMBERS

THROW-INS

6.7 THROW-INS PER GAME WERE IN THE ATTACKING THIRD

T° TEAMS TAKE ON AVERAGE 19.6 THROW-INS PER GAME. (20/21 PL SEASON)

All data by Stats Perform

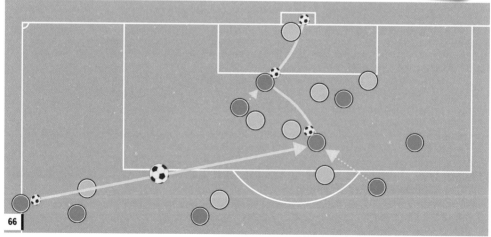

**Coaching throw-ins takes two forms.** First, there is the **technical aspect**. Liverpool hired Thomas Gronnemark, a world-record holder for throw-in length, to teach its players how to maximize distance and flatten trajectory for added speed. Done well, a throw-in can be as effective as a whipped cross.

The second aspect is the same as in any other set piece: **the other players' off-the-ball movement and positioning.** Here, astute teams will assess the opposition's defensive shapes and try to figure out ways for their players to escape from their markers in the box or find dangerous positions just outside it. As with free kicks or corners, this kind of preparation is key to making effective use of good attacking opportunities.

**COACHED WELL, THE HUMBLE THROW-IN IS MORE THAN JUST A MEANS OF RESTARTING THE GAME – IT CAN BECOME A POTENT WEAPON.**

# 16

# LOOK FOR THE SPACE

An explanation of the
corridor of uncertainty

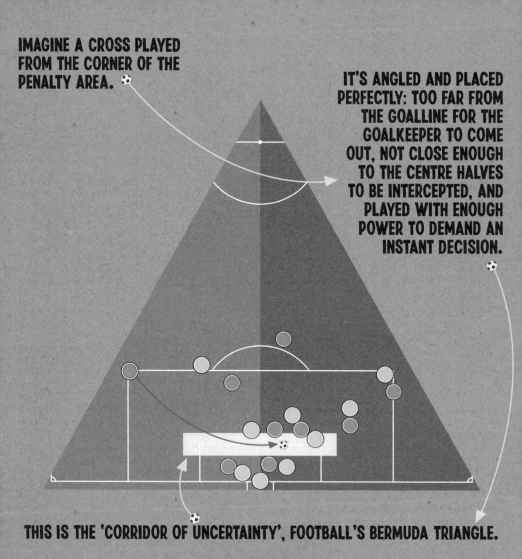

IMAGINE A CROSS PLAYED FROM THE CORNER OF THE PENALTY AREA.

IT'S ANGLED AND PLACED PERFECTLY: TOO FAR FROM THE GOALLINE FOR THE GOALKEEPER TO COME OUT, NOT CLOSE ENOUGH TO THE CENTRE HALVES TO BE INTERCEPTED, AND PLAYED WITH ENOUGH POWER TO DEMAND AN INSTANT DECISION.

THIS IS THE 'CORRIDOR OF UNCERTAINTY', FOOTBALL'S BERMUDA TRIANGLE.

– ALL THREE PLAYERS ARE AN EQUAL DISTANCE FROM THE BALL

## THE POSITION OF THE BALL IS WHAT MATTERS.

By being equidistant from all the defenders **(A)**, it becomes very difficult to know whose responsibility it is to make the clearance, if a clearance is even possible.

The corridor of uncertainty is so potent because not only does it breed hesitation, but also the players charged with removing the threat are typically forced into bad positions – facing their own goal, for instance, or off-balance and with centre forwards close by.

**So, when a ball is played into the corridor, what happens?**

Anything, and that's really the point. A panicked centre half might dangle a leg and inadvertently deflect the ball into his own net. The keeper might have an instinctive flap at the ball or fumble it in a dangerous area. Or an attacking forward might get just enough of a touch to create a further degree of chaos or even score a goal.

It goes without saying that most crosses are played towards a specific target. A hulking targetman, perhaps, or penalty-area predator. Sometimes, though, the best ball is one aimed at no one at all, which teases opportunities for the attacking side and invites the defenders to be rash and impulsive and react to a situation that doesn't have a training-ground response.

## IF ALL ELSE FAILS, FIND THE CORRIDOR OF UNCERTAINTY.

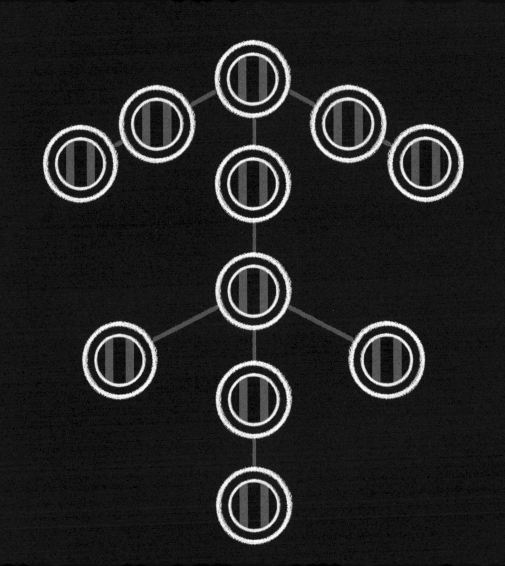

# 17

# KNOW YOUR INFLUENCES:
## HELENIO HERRERA
### (1910–1997)

When defence
ruled the world

## THE ARGENTINE-FRENCH FOOTBALLER AND MANAGER HELENIO HERRERA ACHIEVED ENORMOUS SUCCESS AT INTER MILAN EMPLOYING A SYSTEM KNOWN AS 'CATENACCIO'.

The Italian word for 'door-bolt', catenaccio has become a byword for defensive, even negative, football, in which the aim is to stifle an opponent, reduce their attacking chances, and then counter-attack once that pressure has been absorbed.

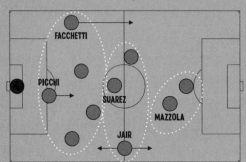

The concept originates in **Karl Rappan's 'verrou', or 'bolt' system**, which was developed in the **1930s and 1940s**, and which saw both wing backs withdrawn to flank the two full backs. This ensured that there was a spare man at the back – **a 'libero' or sweeper.** Herrera's Inter won the European Cup in 1964 and 1965, and were beaten finalists in 1967, losing to Jock Stein's Celtic.

The system looked like a lop-sided 5-3-2, with the left back **Giacinto Facchetti** pushing up aggressively, while the right winger, **Jair,** would move up and down the pitch, covering the space on the right. This was necessary because the right back tucked in to create a back three, with a sweeper, **Armando Picchi,** the last man. **Luis Suárez** (not to be confused with the modern-day Luis Suárez) sat in front of this solid unit, using his immense passing range to initiate sweeping counters, with Facchetti bursting high on the left and scoring frequently.

**Herrera's success with such a clear tactical blueprint means that he's probably associated with a distinct tactical style more than any other manager in history.** He was a strict disciplinarian and began the tradition of the 'ritiro', a pre-game retreat in which players are sequestered at training grounds.

His more lasting legacy might be in the perception of Italian football, however, which is still seen as cautious and defensively oriented. That's a misconception; the modern style is bold and full of goals.

NEVERTHELESS, SUCH WAS HERRERA'S CULTURAL IMPACT THAT CATENACCIO REMAINS APPARENTLY INEXTRICABLE FROM ITALIAN FOOTBALL'S REPUTATION.

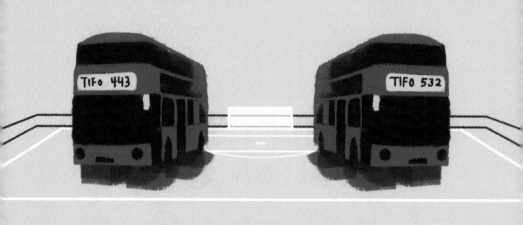

# 18

# SOMETIMES TWO BUSES COME ALONG AT ONCE

## Why some teams funnel shots instead of blocking them

IN 2004, A DISGRUNTLED JOSÉ MOURINHO – AT THE TIME, CHELSEA MANAGER – FIRST INTRODUCED THE ANGLOPHONE WORLD TO THE CONCEPT OF 'PARKING THE BUS', USING IT TO DERIDE A PARTICULARLY NEGATIVE TOTTENHAM PERFORMANCE AT STAMFORD BRIDGE. MOURINHO WAS ACCUSING SPURS OF SHOWING NO AMBITION, OF BEING CYNICAL – AND THAT SENTIMENT HAS BECOME THE EXPRESSION'S ASSOCIATION.

It's also seen as a simple tactic that is easy to execute, with players instructed to sit deep in a **low block (A)**, to play narrowly and to limit the space between their lines. In essence, that's right, but it involves no little craft.

To cede possession is to also cede space. A side in a low block aims to let the opposition have the ball, but only in certain areas. For instance, allowing space in wide positions may encourage crosses into the box, but only from unfavourable angles and towards a tightly packed area **(B)**. Equally, while the low block can give forwards time to shoot, those shots tend to be taken outside the box, or in areas where scoring isn't likely.

In both instances, the team is **controlling the quality of the chance.**

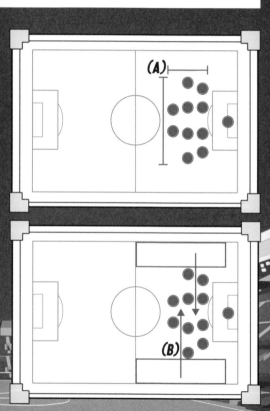

During their long spell in the Premier League, Sean Dyche's Burnley were very good at this, also adding a layer of complexity. Dyche's centre halves and deep midfielders were routinely among those making the highest number of blocks in the Premier League each season, and that was by design – Burnley's approach was **to encourage shots to be taken from positions that were well protected by blockers.**

Dyche also coached his centre backs to take up positions that encouraged particular types of shot, **creating a narrow shooting channel – or funnel – towards the goalkeeper.**

## HENCE PARKING TWO BUSES INSTEAD OF ONE.

The result is a lot of shots conceded, but of the type that the keeper or other covering defenders are able to deal with without conceding goals.

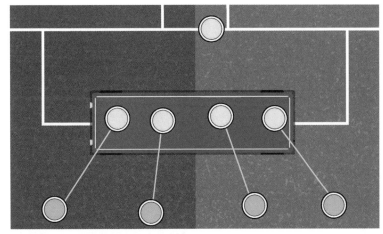

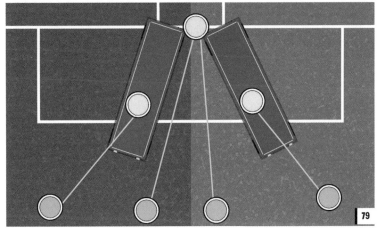

79

# 19

# THE TOUCHLINE IS A DEFENDER

## Use space effectively when defending

**THE LESS SPACE AN OPPONENT HAS, THE EASIER IT IS TO DEFEND AGAINST THEM. BUT DEFENDING ISN'T ALWAYS REACTIONARY; SOMETIMES, TEAMS MANUFACTURE SITUATIONS THAT ALLOW THEM A BETTER CHANCE OF WINNING THE BALL.**

**'PRESSING TRIGGERS' ARE A GOOD EXAMPLE.**

**Pressing is the concerted and structured effort to win back possession by chasing and closing down the opposition.**

It relies upon 'triggers'. These are events within a game that literally 'trigger' the press – they're a series of coaching instructions that let players know when to move towards the ball or player in possession.

A very common pressing trigger is the ball being passed to a player near the touchline, and there's a simple reason for this. Players need passing options; next to the touchline, however, most of a player's possible angles are shut down.

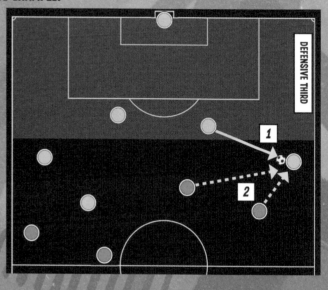

**The touchline is acting as another defender,** effectively making sure that the player in possession can only pass away from it, or else concede a throw-in.

This is obviously especially dangerous if the player receiving the pass is in their own **defensive third,** because a throw-in there can be a weapon for the attacking team. Teams that press high look to squeeze the opposition towards the touchline, hemming them in. The player being pressed then either kicks it out or must make a dangerous pass infield where the opposition have more players hunting the ball. If they win it, then they can transition into attack.

Of course, very good sides can exploit this, by playing towards the touchline, drawing the opposition to one side of the pitch, but then playing a long pass to the other, more open, side. But this is hard to do and requires enormous skill and some bravery, with long balls across the pitch risking interceptions in dangerous areas. **For most teams, it's far better to avoid playing close to the line, thereby depriving the opposition of another defender.**

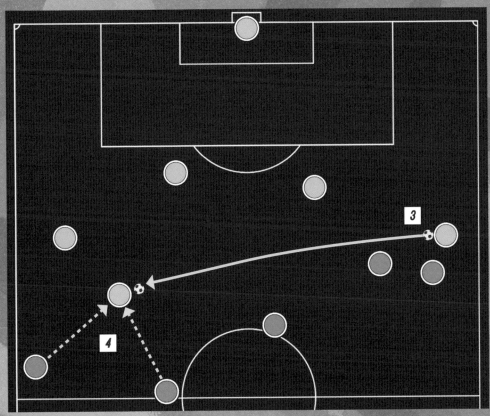

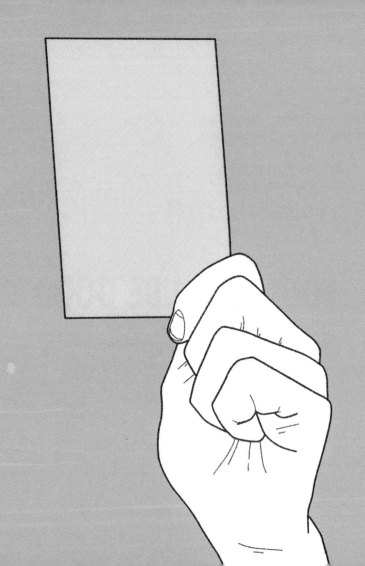

# 20

# FOULS CAN BE GOOD

The rise of tactical fouling
in modern football

**ARE FOULS TO BE AVOIDED? WELL, NOT ALWAYS. SOMETIMES THEY'RE PART OF A TEAM'S STRATEGY AND A NECESSARY MEANS BY WHICH THEY PROTECT THEMSELVES. AND, WHILE NOT CONFINED TO THE BIG CLUBS, IT'S PARTICULARLY TRUE OF THOSE SIDES WHO ENJOY A LOT OF POSSESSION AND TERRITORY.**

For instance, when attacking, **Pep Guardiola's teams** have tended to organize themselves into a 2-3-5 shape. It creates a lot of advantageous numerical mismatches in attack, but in the event of a turnover – when the ball is lost, or won by the opposition – it can expose their remaining defensive players and leave them short-handed.

To minimize that danger, a player – often a deep midfielder – is assigned the responsibility of breaking up anything that develops. It was **Sergio Busquets** at Barcelona, **Javi Martínez** at Bayern Munich and – for a long time – **Fernandinho** at Manchester City.

Of course, the responsibility also lies with other players, but the idea is clear enough: to disrupt a move before it begins, with the kind of soft fouls that rarely draw yellow cards. A tug of the shirt, perhaps, or a little trip.

And Guardiola's Manchester City are very good at that – even if the stats don't always show it.

In the 2018–19 season, for instance, which ended with City winning the Premier League, they committed 328 fouls, the second fewest in the competition. But with context, the pattern – and tactic – becomes clearer.

City averaged 67.8% possession that season, meaning that those 328 fouls occurred during the 32.2% of the time spent without the ball. On average, the ball is in play for roughly 60 minutes of each Premier League, meaning that – in that season at least – City's 328 fouls, or 8.6 per game, were condensed into the 20 minutes of each game that they spent without the ball while it was in play – **the equivalent of one every 140 seconds.**

**Watford** committed 483 fouls that season. At 12.7 per game, that was the division's highest. But they also averaged just 44.3% possession. Using our sketched formula which adjusts for the time the ball actually spent in play, that gives an average of around 33 minutes each game that Watford spent out of possession, meaning that they committed a foul – roughly – every 156 seconds without the ball. **Watford committed more fouls, but Manchester City fouled more frequently.**

(There are caveats. A team doesn't only commit fouls without the ball and, of course, our working here is rough. It's just an outline, but it still provides a new perspective.)

The deliberate foul is a controversial tactic, because it can be seen as cynical and as preventing the kind of transitions from which scoring chances – and attractive football – so often result, but it remains a legitimate tool for teams looking to guard against quick breaks.

# 21

# SOMETIMES, LYING DOWN ON THE JOB IS GOOD

The phenomenon of draft excluders

**IN 2018, DURING A CHAMPIONS LEAGUE GROUP-STAGE MATCH AT BARCELONA'S CAMP NOU, INTER MILAN'S MARCELO BROZOVIĆ BEGAN A TREND THAT SUBSEQUENTLY SPREAD THROUGH THE GAME LIKE WILDFIRE.**

**Brozović's Inter** were facing a free kick on the edge of their own box and at the last minute, guessing that **Luis Suárez** was about to aim his shot under the defensive wall as it jumped, the Croatian flung himself to the ground behind his teammates and successfully deflected the ball over the crossbar.

It wasn't the very first time this had happened, but it was the point at which it became universally adopted. **Now it's rare to see a defensive wall constructed without a player lying behind it – without a 'draught excluder'.** Yes, it now has a name, which is near proof that it's here to stay.

To some it's still a fad, but then that ignores the clear logic behind it. A virtual seal at the base of the defensive wall takes away the opportunity for a low, trick-shot free kick that is particularly effective from close range. Suárez has done it before and, among others, Brazilian legend **Ronaldinho** also had it in his repertoire. What's more, the draught excluder should also allow the standing players in the wall to focus on what they're there for, which is to jump as high as possible and not worry about being caught out as they do.

**And that's never more important than it is from within 25 yards, because the higher the wall jumps, the more difficult the technique required to get the ball up and over the defenders, but then down in time to find the net. With the draught excluder also removing the low route to the goal – which might well have been the easier avenue – scoring from close-range free kicks just became much harder.**

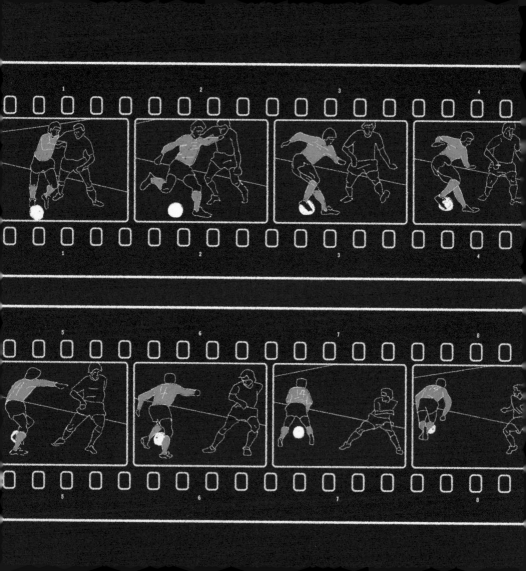

# 22

# KNOW YOUR INFLUENCES:
## JOHAN CRUYFF
## (1947–2016)

The Godfather
of Barcelona

## IT'S PROBABLY NOT AN EXAGGERATION TO SAY THAT NO ONE MAN HAS HAD SUCH A WIDESPREAD AND SUCCESSFUL INFLUENCE IN FOOTBALL AS JOHAN CRUYFF.

**As a player, Cruyff epitomized the all-conquering and innovative Ajax and Netherlands sides of the 1970s.** They pressed hard, perfected positional rotations, and employed a libero: a centre back who swept forwards into midfield to carry the ball and add an extra player to the central three, turning Cruyff's preferred 4-3-3 into a 3-4-3.

While Cruyff was the nation's best player, he was also a cultural icon. Talismanic and talented, Cruyff was never shy when it came to sharing his opinions on football or anything else. He pushed for better pay and sponsorship deals for players and was one of the first to understand the commercial potential of being a world-class footballer.

His move into management was probably even more significant. Cruyff's spell in charge of **Barcelona**, a club where he had won **La Liga** and his second and third **Ballons d'Or** as a player, laid the groundwork for so much. Cruyff stressed technicality over physicality, removing the height requirements at La Masia, Barcelona's training academy, to ensure that players like **Andrés Iniesta** could later prosper. This emphasis meant he could reshape his **Dutch Total Football** into what we now call **positional play,** which reached its peak in **Spain's global footballing dominance between 2008 and 2012.**

*Between 2008 and 2012, Spain won two European Championships and one World Cup, while Barcelona won three La Liga titles and two Champions Leagues.*

Cruyff instilled a combination of relentless desire for improvement and a commitment to attacking football that would become the hallmark of Barcelona in the following decades, giving the world perhaps the best club side ever seen between 2008 and 2012 under his protégé **Pep Guardiola.** He famously earmarked Guardiola as a talent while watching Barcelona's B team, then built his European Cup-winning side around the midfielder.

TO THIS DAY, DESPITE HIS DEATH IN 2016, CRUYFF AND HIS IDEALS REMAIN A REFERENCE POINT FOR THE WAY BARCELONA'S YOUNG PLAYERS ARE COACHED AND THE WAY ITS TEAMS PLAY.

# 23

# FOOTBALL CLUBS ARE BUSINESSES

Understanding the three
main revenue streams

# THE WAYS IN WHICH FOOTBALL CLUBS MAKE MONEY HAVE DEVELOPED OVER TIME.

The scale of income varies enormously, of course, and reflects the size, appeal and visibility of individual clubs, but methods of making money are fairly consistent and can be divided into **three categories, or three streams of income: matchday, commercial and broadcasting.**

**MATCHDAY INCOME is the revenue a club makes from staging games.** So, that would include ticket sales, and the money made from corporate hospitality and even the cups of tea sold on the concourses around the ground. As a general rule, the bigger a team's stadium, the more money they'll make from it, and – because new stadium builds and major renovation projects are rare – the amount a club makes season-to-season tends to be much the same.

**COMMERCIAL INCOME** is more variable. **This includes everything a club makes from sponsorship agreements:** the brands and logos displayed on shirts, the licence to produce and sell matchday and training kit – commonly known as a manufacturing deal – and also any official partnerships the club establishes with companies from different industrial sectors. **Manchester United**, for instance, currently have an official wine partner, an official vision partner and an official mattress and pillow partner.

No single factor determines how profitable this area can be. Instead, it's really a blend of on-field performance, historic success and – in some cases – global reach. Particularly famous players are relevant, too, and their image can certainly influence both the size of the financial commitment a sponsor is willing to make, the type of organization they're likely to be, and what geographical location they trade in.

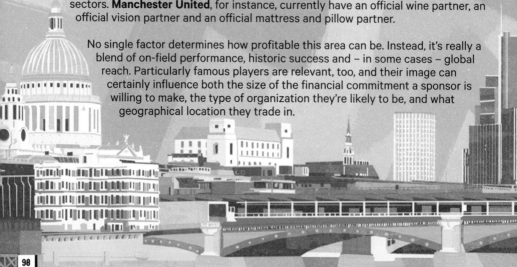

**BROADCASTING INCOME** is the third revenue stream, and it is among the most contentious topics in football. Broadcasting income refers to the amount of money a club makes from selling its television rights. For the biggest teams, that's income drawn from more than one competition – the domestic league and domestic cups, but also its participation and progress in European tournaments, like the **Champions League**, for which teams qualify via their finishing position in the league, or by winning certain trophies.

It's controversial because it varies from league to league. **The Premier League** has the richest broadcasting contract in world football, valued at around £1.6bn each season, and 50% is shared evenly between its member teams. In other countries, however, most notably in Spain, the overall value of the contract is not only considerably less – around half, at £854m – but it also greatly favours the traditionally strong teams, helping to consolidate their position. At the end of the 2020–21 season, first-placed **Barcelona** earned €165.6m from **La Liga's** television broadcasting contract, while last-placed **Huesca** received just €46.8m.

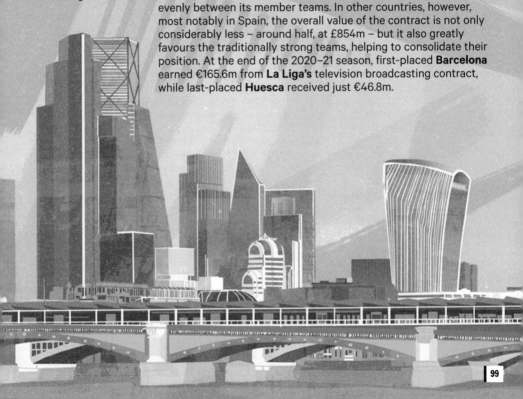

# 24

# YOUTH ACADEMIES ARE BUSINESS MODELS

Football's production
line explained

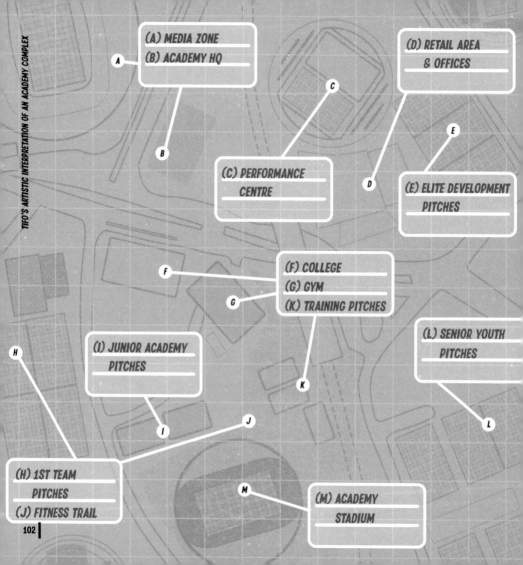

TIFO'S ARTISTIC INTERPRETATION OF AN ACADEMY COMPLEX

(A) MEDIA ZONE

(B) ACADEMY HQ

(D) RETAIL AREA
& OFFICES

(C) PERFORMANCE
CENTRE

(E) ELITE DEVELOPMENT
PITCHES

(F) COLLEGE

(G) GYM

(K) TRAINING PITCHES

(L) SENIOR YOUTH
PITCHES

(I) JUNIOR ACADEMY
PITCHES

(H) 1ST TEAM
PITCHES

(J) FITNESS TRAIL

(M) ACADEMY
STADIUM

**IN DECEMBER 2014, MANCHESTER CITY OPENED BRAND NEW TRAINING FACILITIES AS PART OF THEIR ETIHAD COMPLEX. THEY INCLUDED NEW PITCHES, HOTEL-STANDARD ACCOMMODATION, STATE OF THE ART VIDEO AUDITORIUMS AND A MINI-STADIUM, WHICH IS USED TO STAGE ACADEMY AND WOMEN'S GAMES.**

The hope – and one of the justifications for the expenditure – was that it would also attract some of the best young players in the world to the club's academy.

Almost eight years later, **Phil Foden** is really the only academy player to have made a true impression on the first team, and he was at the club long before ground was broken in 2014.

But that doesn't mean that the project's aims haven't been met.

Academies exist to create footballers, that's certainly true. A better way of looking at it, however, is to see those footballers as assets who either have value to **Manchester City** or who can be loaned or sold to provide a valuable additional source of revenue. Football clubs are businesses, and creating footballers is part of the way they function in their industry.

In 2018, for instance, City sold **Angus Gunn, Pablo Maffeo, Jason Denayer** and **Brahim Díaz** for collective fees of around £43m. Twelve months earlier, **Enes Ünal** and **Kelechi Iheanacho** had departed for around £37m combined and, between 2019 and the present day, **Douglas Luiz, Angeliño, Lukas Nmecha** and **Jack Harrison** have all been sold, raising a further £50m.

**All ten of those players joined the club as teenagers** and whether or not they played for the first team is effectively incidental. Some arrived before the facilities were upgraded, others joined afterwards and, perhaps, partly because of them. Together, however, they represent a flow of talent from City's academy into the professional game and a return of £130m, and that figure doesn't include income from the minor players who were also traded during the same period.

Given that the cost of that 2014 upgrade was some £200m, it seems quite likely that the expanded Etihad Complex has paid for itself in less than a decade, and helped to provide the club with a vital fourth source of revenue beyond commercial revenue from sponsorship and merchandising sales, and matchday and broadcasting income.

**SO, JUST BECAUSE AN ACADEMY ISN'T STOCKING A CLUB'S FIRST TEAM DOESN'T MEAN THAT IT ISN'T PRODUCING FOOTBALLERS FOR SOMEONE.**

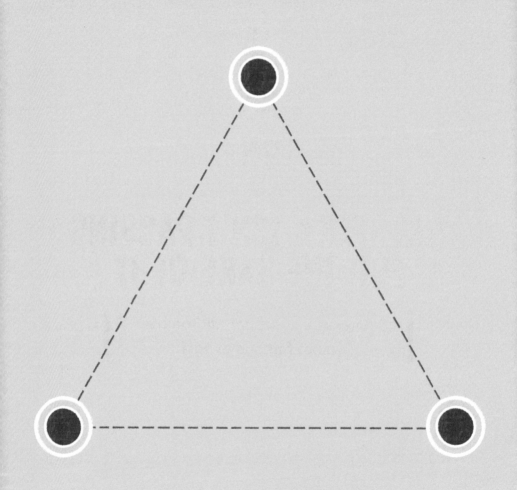

# 25

# TIKI-TAKA ISN'T PASSING FOR THE SAKE OF IT

The true definition of Spain's
most famous export

## 'TIKI-TAKA' IS ALL ABOUT KEEPING AND PASSING THE BALL. IT'S A STYLE OF PLAY THAT TREASURES POSSESSION AND PATIENCE.

**But that's not all it is.** Tiki-taka is associated with some of the finest teams in modern history and some of the most thrilling football ever played – just think of Pep Guardiola's Barcelona.

Possession is a starting point – a foundation block. By controlling the ball and circulating it in short, sharp patterns, a team not only keeps it away from their opponent but is also able to build a secure defensive structure at the same time, protecting themselves should possession be lost.

So far, so simple. But the key to its effectiveness is quality in execution and a set of abilities that most sides just don't have. It needs the brilliant timing and exemplary technique of players capable of transforming a situation with just one or two touches.

Some teams prefer to get the ball forward with as few passes as possible. Others want to move the ball wide for their wingers. By contrast, **tiki-taka's attacking aim is to use its blend of precise passing, perfect movement and rapid ball circulation to create and exploit space, to produce the numerical mismatches in areas from which good goalscoring opportunities arise.**

## MOVE IT, MOVE IT, AND MOVE IT AGAIN, KEEP TEASING AND STRETCHING THE OPPOSITION UNTIL THEIR DEFENSIVE SHAPE BREAKS. THAT'S THE MINDSET.

Guardiola's Barcelona was uniquely equipped to do that, constructed as it was from homegrown La Masia graduates, all of whom had been trained since childhood to play in that distinctive one- or two-touch style and who, crucially, were raised on the principles of 'positional play' at the root of the club's technical identity.

Without those players and that execution, with missing ingredients, it would have been passing for passing's sake and would have lacked the incisiveness to be so successful.

## TIFO EXPLAINS: POSITIONAL PLAY

**Positional play** is a guiding principle for many top sides. It's based on a series of ideas that might be quite simple, but which are still very difficult to coach.

**Pep Guardiola** is its most famous contemporary practitioner, and his teaching method involves **dividing a training pitch into different zones, using horizontal and vertical lines, and then teaching players when and where to move depending on where the ball, their teammates, or their opponents are.**

The grid comes with rules, too. There should never be more than three players on the same horizontal line, or two on the same vertical line and the expectation – eventually – is for players to instinctively know when and where to move.

It's demanding of players. Intellectually, of course, but also because – by its nature – positional play involves a lot of rotation and needs players to be comfortable in several different positions as they rotate in and out of zones. **The aim, though, is to create one of three different types of superiority.**

**Numerical superiority** is much as it sounds and involves having more players than an opponent in a particular area of the pitch. **Qualitative superiority** is more subtle. It's the creation of a technical or physical advantage: a quick player against a slow one, for instance, or a tall attacker against a small defender. Finally, **positional superiority** is about getting players into particular areas, perhaps between a line or beyond a defence, with the aim of giving them time on the ball or the opportunity to score or create a goal.

POSITONAL PLAY RULES!

THERE SHOULD NEVER BE MORE THAN THREE PLAYERS ON THE SAME HORIZONTAL LINE, OR TWO ON THE SAME VERTICAL LINE!

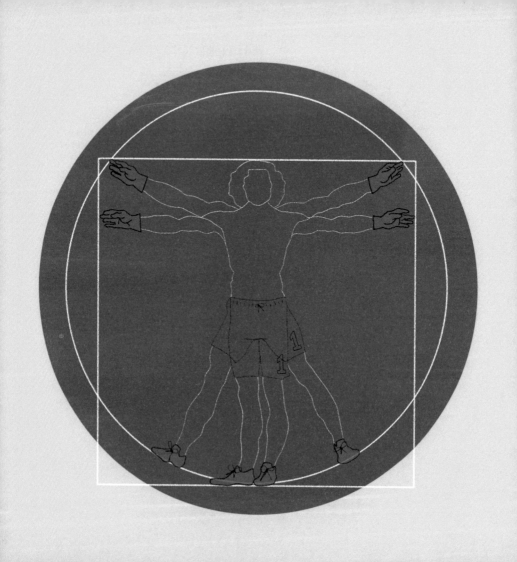

# 26

# GOALKEEPERS' FEET ARE IMPORTANT

The modern goalkeeper
as a playmaker

# WHEN YOU THINK OF GOALKEEPERS, YOU THINK OF THEIR HANDS. THEIRS IS THE ONLY POSITION THAT CAN USE THEM, AFTER ALL. BUT, INCREASINGLY, A KEEPER'S FEET ARE ALMOST AS IMPORTANT.

**Defensively,** having a goalkeeper with good feet matters, because good footwork is crucial for making saves. Keepers like **Manuel Neuer, David de Gea and Petr Cech** – a former ice hockey keeper – also use their legs and feet brilliantly to stop goals. A keeper with real control and passing ability can easily intercept balls outside the penalty area, allowing their team to play higher up the pitch and further away from their own goal. This usefully compresses the space in which the opposition can play.

**Offensively,** it can be even more effective, as **Johan Cruyff** knew: he wanted his goalkeeper to be his first attacker (and his attackers to be his first defenders). A goalkeeper with an excellent passing range can help teams build from the back, drawing the opposition towards them to create space elsewhere. They can offer a good passing option, too, which means less lumping it forwards and surrendering possession. And the best can carve through the opposition lines with raking low passes, or carefully chipped balls towards the sidelines, distributing with the skill of a central midfielder.

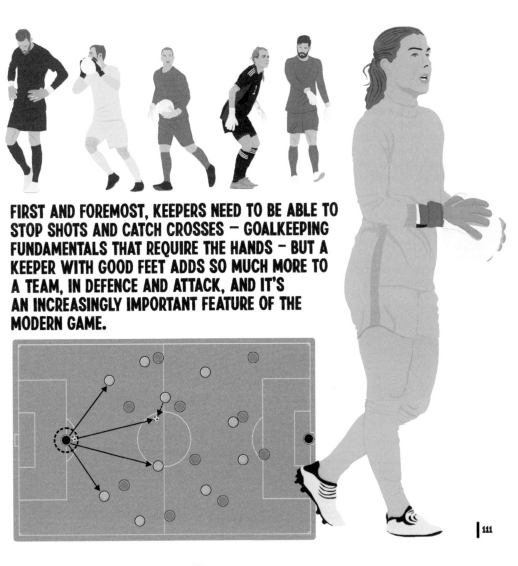

FIRST AND FOREMOST, KEEPERS NEED TO BE ABLE TO STOP SHOTS AND CATCH CROSSES – GOALKEEPING FUNDAMENTALS THAT REQUIRE THE HANDS – BUT A KEEPER WITH GOOD FEET ADDS SO MUCH MORE TO A TEAM, IN DEFENCE AND ATTACK, AND IT'S AN INCREASINGLY IMPORTANT FEATURE OF THE MODERN GAME.

## 27

# OBSERVE THE HALF-SPACE

## The most dangerous area of the pitch explained

# IN ORDER TO OBSERVE THE HALF-SPACE, YOU FIRST NEED TO KNOW WHERE IT IS.

The term comes from German coaching theory and was popularized by Austrian coach **René Marić**. The pitch is divided end-to-end into **five channels, one central, two wide, and between them, the two half-spaces.**

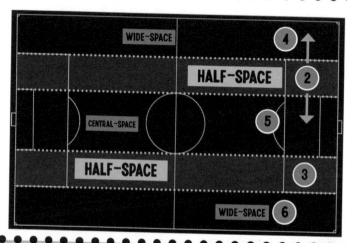

IT'S EASY TO THINK THE HALF-SPACES ARE FIXED IN WIDTH BUT THEY MAY SHIFT DEPENDING ON WHERE THE OPPOSITION DEFENDERS ARE.

## WHY IS THE HALF-SPACE WORTH OBSERVING?

Getting players free on the ball in the half-spaces wins games, as they can often generate better chances from those zones. Part of the reason for this is to do with **angles**.

If a player is **wide (A)**, they have a touchline behind them – meaning they can't pass or move in that direction – and they are relatively far from the goal. A cross from this position must be of a high quality to reach a teammate.

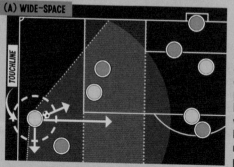

(A) WIDE-SPACE

TOUCHLINE

**Centrally (B)**, an attacker is nearer the goal and has a wide array of passing angles, but the centre of a pitch is always the most congested part. Forward passes also often need to be played to a teammate with their back to goal, because the pass is moving straight up the pitch.

114

In the **half-space (C)**, though, we find the best of both worlds. It's less busy, so there's more time to pick a pass. A player is not next to the touchline, so retains the option to pass wide, making passing options more difficult to defend.

And the angles mean a player is close to goal but can also play passes that cut in behind defenders, or meet runs from a player who can move forwards on to the pass. And their proximity to teammates and the goal means there is far less time for defenders to react.

**IF AN ATTACKING TEAM CAN OCCUPY THE HALF-SPACE, THEY WILL FIND IT FAR EASIER TO GENERATE HIGH-QUALITY CHANCES.**

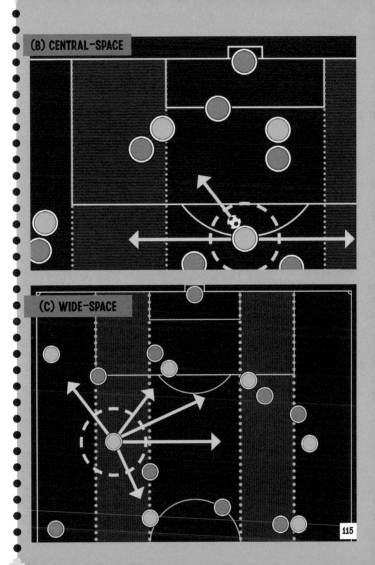

(B) CENTRAL-SPACE

(C) WIDE-SPACE

# 28

# PASS COMPLETION DOESN'T MATTER

How to better understand statistics
and *which ones* make a difference

## PASS COMPLETION PERCENTAGES ARE AMONG THE MOST MISLEADING STATISTICS IN THE GAME.

They may tell you that a player has successfully passed the ball to a teammate, but not what it achieves within a game. Nor does it really describe a player's abilities in any meaningful way.

Data application is still in its football infancy, but it's already at a stage at which it's able to properly contextualize passing and solve some of these problems.

Instead of raw completion percentages, we're now able to look at, for instance, how many **progressive passes** a player makes.

## A PROGRESSIVE PASS IS ONE THAT MOVES THE BALL TEN YARDS OR MORE CLOSER TO THE OPPONENTS' GOAL, AND IT IS A USEFUL MEASURE OF PLAYMAKING ABILITY.

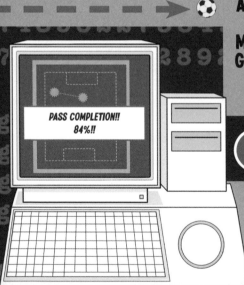

PASS COMPLETION!!
84%!!

10 YARDS = 9.14 METRES

Or we can look at **passes under pressure** – how many times a player passes the ball while being hassled. Given how ubiquitous pressing is in the modern game, that's a particularly valuable way of judging how well a player copes with intensive, off-the-ball pressure.

**At the very least, it's always important to know what kind of passes a player is completing.**

There's clearly a difference between a centre half who spends the game pushing five-yard passes around with perfect accuracy and one who, for example, is completing at a lower percentage but consistently moves the ball over long distances and in a way that actually changes the game. With a long diagonal pass to a winger, perhaps, or a quick, well-flighted ball over the top of a defence.

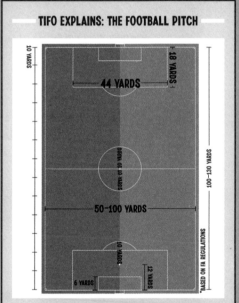

TIFO EXPLAINS: THE FOOTBALL PITCH

10 YARDS

18 YARDS

44 YARDS

20 YARDS TO 10 YARDS

100–130 YARDS

50–100 YARDS

*BASED ON FA REGULATIONS

10 YARDS

12 YARDS

6 YARDS

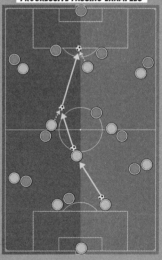

PROGRESSIVE PASSING EXAMPLES

**THERE'S NOTHING INHERENTLY WRONG WITH PASS COMPLETION AS AN ANECDOTAL STATISTIC, BUT IT DOESN'T REALLY DESCRIBE PLAYERS, THEIR ABILITIES OR THE MATCH THEY'RE PLAYING IN.**

# 29

# KNOW YOUR INFLUENCES:
## ARRIGO SACCHI
## (1946-)

The son of
a shoe salesman

## ARRIGO SACCHI REVOLUTIONIZED ITALIAN FOOTBALL.

**INTO AN ENVIRONMENT THAT HAD BECOME DEFENSIVELY ORIENTED, MAYBE EVEN FEARFUL AND PASSIVE, HE BROUGHT AN AGGRESSIVE, MORE ATTACKING STYLE OF PLAY. HIS INFLUENCE ON THE REST OF EUROPE WAS IMMENSE, TOO. HE STARTED COACHING WHILE STILL WORKING AT HIS FATHER'S SHOE FACTORY AND FAMOUSLY NEVER PLAYED PROFESSIONALLY. ONCE CRITICIZED FOR HIS LACK OF PLAYING EXPERIENCE, HE RESPONDED, 'I NEVER REALIZED THAT TO BE A JOCKEY YOU HAD TO BE A HORSE FIRST.'**

He rose quickly through Italian football management but he's most remembered for his time at **AC Milan. Silvio Berlusconi** had bought the club in **1986** and wanted to revive it, handing the reins to the attack-minded Sacchi.

Sacchi was inspired by the **Real Madrid side of the 1950s** and **Rinus Michels' 1970s Ajax** teams. He played with a back four, unusual in Italy at the time, and organized his side to mark zonally rather than man-to-man. **He famously believed that every player should think about their positioning four ways: in relation to the ball, to space, to their teammates, and to the opposition.** His teams pressed ferociously by the standards of the time,

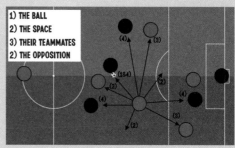

1) THE BALL
2) THE SPACE
3) THEIR TEAMMATES
2) THE OPPOSITION

and he achieved this by insisting on vertical compactness: **there should never be more than 25 metres between the defenders and the strikers when in a defensive posture.**

Sacchi was a hugely articulate advocate of attacking play and had strong ideas about coaching the game. He felt that too much attention was paid to the player in possession and too little to how players move off the ball. He brought in the idea of **shadow-play,** coaching structures in training without a ball or an opposition, to ensure that his teams got their positioning right.

Shadow-play sounds like a strange idea, but it worked. Sacchi would assemble all eleven of his players on a full-sized pitch, tell them where the imaginary ball was, and then watch as they mimicked passing it to one another or pressing an invisible opponent, with every player moving into a position defined by a corresponding action. It remains a curious phenomenon to watch, but it's a very effective way of drilling a team to the point at which knowing where to be at all times, with or without the ball, becomes second-nature.

SACCHI PROVED IT BY WINNING TWO EUROPEAN CUPS WITH AC MILAN, AND HIS INFLUENCE LEFT ITS MARK ON — AMONG MANY OTHERS — CONTEMPORARY MANAGERS LIKE JÜRGEN KLOPP, JOSÉ MOURINHO AND ANTONIO CONTE.

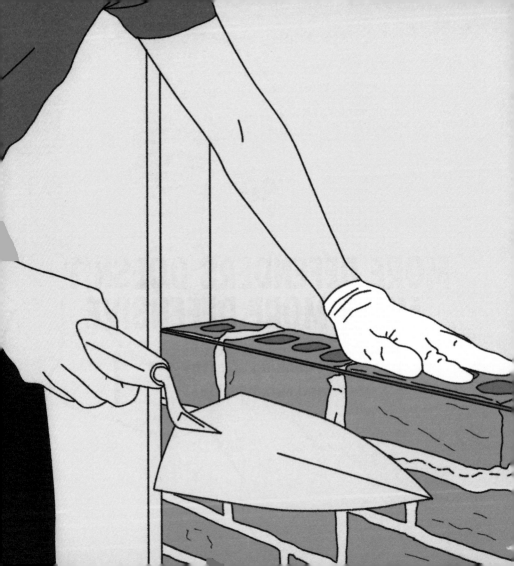

# 30

# MORE DEFENDERS DOESN'T MEAN MORE DEFENSIVE

### Rethinking strategy and substitutions

YOU CAN HEAR THE GROANS AS A MIDFIELDER, OR WORSE STILL AN ATTACKER, IS SUBSTITUTED FOR ANOTHER CENTRE BACK. IT WILL MAKE US MORE DEFENSIVE, WE'LL INVITE PRESSURE, WE'LL CONCEDE: THESE ARE THE OBVIOUS CONCERNS THAT ANY FAN WATCHING MIGHT HAVE SHOULD THEIR MANAGER MAKE SUCH A CHANGE DURING A GAME.

(A)

THE FIRST LINE OF THE PRESS

But bringing on an additional centre back shouldn't always be seen as **parking the bus.** In fact, switching to a back three, for instance, can have positive attacking outcomes.

**First,** an additional defender allows for a shape change that can make it easier to play out from the back, since having three centre backs naturally causes wing backs to move higher up the pitch. Unless the opposition adjusts its system, this can mean that it's easier to bypass the first wave of **the pressing opponents (A).** As well as having more players further up the pitch, higher wing backs can also pin back the opposition full backs or tie up their wingers, which again makes ball progression easier.

**Second,** centre backs have their own attacking value. Some can **play long passes into the wide channels** of the pitch **(B)**, perhaps for those newly advanced wing backs, or hit long balls to a striker. But they can also **carry the ball forwards themselves**; many modern defenders are skilful.

With two colleagues as security, the spare centre back can stride forwards **(C)**, pushing the opposition lines back and becoming, effectively, an additional midfielder. This **libero-like quality** is safer coming from a back three, but also means that removing a midfielder doesn't lead to fewer bodies in that part of the pitch.

**NEXT TIME YOUR MANAGER BRINGS ON ANOTHER CENTRE BACK, JUST REMEMBER: IT COULD ACTUALLY BE AN ATTACKING MOVE.**

# 31

# LEARN THE LAW

The importance
of loopholes

# THE BOSMAN RULING CHANGED FOOTBALL PLAYERS' RELATIONSHIPS WITH CLUBS FOR EVER. IT IS A WIDELY UNDERSTOOD TURNING POINT IN THE SPORT'S MODERN HISTORY.

It occurred during a precedent-setting legal challenge from little-known Belgian footballer **Jean-Marc Bosman**. Previously, clubs had claimed that they retained certain rights to players even after the expiration of their contracts – which meant that the club could still demand transfer fees for them or otherwise prevent them from joining a new team. The Bosman ruling changed all that: **players could move freely once their contracts ended and with no compensation due to their former employer.**

## LESS KNOWN IS THE WEBSTER RULING, A SELDOM-USED CLAUSE IN THE TRANSFER REGULATIONS.

**Heart of Midlothian's centre back Andy Webster** was central to the side finishing second in the **Scottish Premier League in 2005–6**. At the end of the season, Webster – who was twelve months away from completing his four-year contract – was ready to make a move.

*SEASON ENDS!*

X **THE ANDY WEBSTER RULING PERIOD** X
(*WITH A FEW CAVEATS!*)

*15 DAYS LATER!*

But, interested parties were unable to reach an agreement with Hearts, who valued him at a steep £4m. So Webster turned to **FIFA,** world football's governing body, and invoked Article 17 of their transfer regulations.

It's a clause that allows a player to **break a contract** if they give notice within fifteen days of a season ending, and so long as three years of that contract has already been served – or two years if the contract was signed at the age of 28 or older.

So Webster informed Hearts that he was leaving to join **Wigan Athletic** and, because Article 17 had been invoked, his transfer fee would be set by FIFA. The formula used to calculate fees in such cases is intentionally vague and involves (but is not limited to) the length of the remaining contract, the original cost of the player to the selling club, and the national laws governing the clubs involved.

## IN THE WEBSTER CASE, HEARTS WERE APPALLED BY THE JUDGEMENT.

FIFA determined that they were owed just £625,000, nowhere near the £4m they'd hoped for. It got worse. On appeal to the **Court of Arbitration for Sport,** that figure was actually reduced to just £150,000, after it was ruled that neither the cost to Hearts of having to replace Webster nor their development of him as a player should be taken into account.

Bad news for Hearts, but not necessarily a precedent. **The Webster ruling has been used sparingly,** and FIFA's tribunal has ruled in favour of the 'selling' club just as often, so it shouldn't be considered the equivalent of a secret release clause, more a strange quirk of the transfer regulations and another waypoint in their evolution.

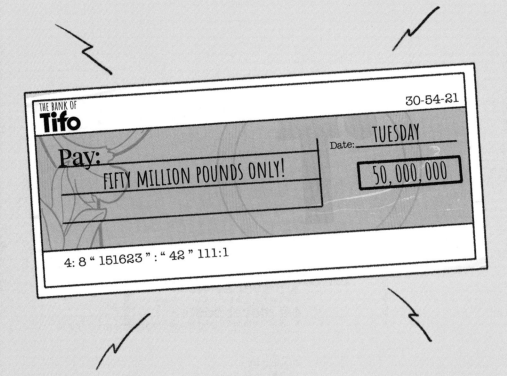

# 32

# TRANSFER FEES ARE MISLEADING

## What a player earns vs what a player costs

NOTES - BUDGET MEETING

## KEY QUESTION!! CAN WE AFFORD TO SIGN THESE PLAYERS?

| | PLAYER ONE | | PLAYER TWO |
|---|---|---|---|
| SAME SIGNING COST (WHICH GOES TO THE SELLING CLUB) | SIGN FOR 50M | | SIGN FOR 50M |
| DIFFERENT WAGE COST (WHICH GOES TO THE PLAYER) | 200K A WEEK X 52<br>10.4M A YEAR | | 100K A WEEK X 52<br>5.2M A YEAR |
| WAGES OVER LIFETIME OF CONTRACT WHICH GOES TO THE PLAYER | X 5 YEARS =<br>£52,000,000 | | X 5 YEARS =<br>£26,000,000 |
| OVERALL COST PAID TO THE SELLING CLUB AND PLAYER | £102 MILLION* | | £76 MILLION* |

2B PENCIL

Whether or not a transfer is seen as a good bit of business is always based on how well a player performs within the context of the original fee paid. Spend £50m, expect £50m worth of goals, assists, tackles and performances. That's what separates a bargain from a flop.

But is that the right way to do it?

Well, no, because a transfer fee is just the cost of buying out an existing contract and bears no relation to the price of actually employing a player once a deal has been struck.

How much that player earns in wages is extremely significant; so too are the hidden fees that don't often get reported. Contracts are usually laden with bonuses, meaning that a player's pay is influenced by performance. Clauses may include incentives relating to playing time and scoring goals, but also performance targets such as finishing in certain league positions or reaching a particular stage of a cup.

So, even our simplified example shows that, despite the original cost of the two players being the same, their club's respective investments – and, consequently, any notion of value for money – are very different. In the example opposite, £26m different, in fact.

Is a player worth their transfer fee? That's really the wrong question to ask. More pertinent is whether a player is worth what they have been, and what they continue to be, paid.

# 33

# NO TRANSFER IS AN ISLAND

| The butterfly effect
of football transfers |

**IN AUGUST 2017, NEYMAR COMPLETED HIS TRANSFER FROM BARCELONA TO PARIS SAINT-GERMAIN FOR A WORLD RECORD £199.8M.**

It set off a chain reaction that continues to shape European football to this day.

Barcelona didn't want to sell Neymar and had no interest in negotiating his departure. That was no obstacle for PSG, though, because they had the financial clout to simply cover his release clause and cut Barça out of the equation.

So began the butterfly effect.

Stung by having such a valuable player snatched away, **Barcelona** quickly – and hastily – reinvested, spending £121.5m apiece on **Borussia Dortmund's Ousmane Dembélé** and, six months later, **Liverpool's Philippe Coutinho**. Both are good players, but under political pressure after Neymar's departure and in need of statement signings, Barcelona's then president **Josep Bartomeu** overpaid for each, beginning a trend that would see the club's transfer efficiency plummet, their wage bill soar, and their debt rise above €1bn.

Meanwhile, **Liverpool** would spend their Coutinho spoils on **Virgil van Dijk** and goalkeeper **Alisson**, the final pieces in a team that would win the **Champions League** and, the following year, the **Premier League** for the first time in the competition's history. On their way to the 2019 Champions League final, Liverpool even managed to complete a miraculous four-goal semi-final comeback against Barcelona, the club who had inadvertently bankrolled their journey to the top of the game.

**Dortmund's** reinvestment wasn't quite so spectacular, but Dembélé's departure freed up a place on the right of their attack, encouraging them – a week after his sale – to take a chance on the young English forward **Jadon Sancho,** who had never played a senior game up to that point, but

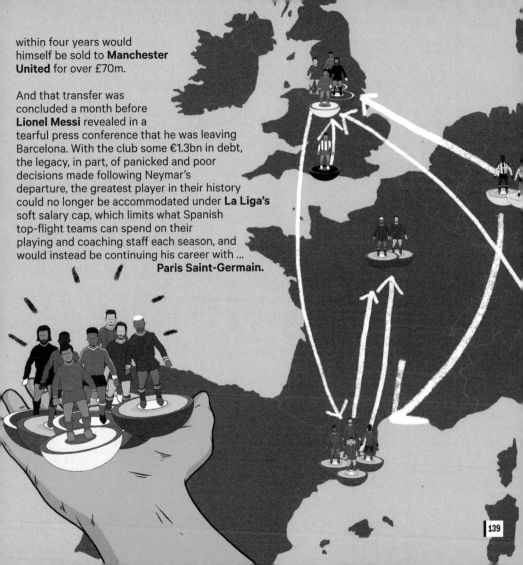

within four years would himself be sold to **Manchester United** for over £70m.

And that transfer was concluded a month before **Lionel Messi** revealed in a tearful press conference that he was leaving Barcelona. With the club some €1.3bn in debt, the legacy, in part, of panicked and poor decisions made following Neymar's departure, the greatest player in their history could no longer be accommodated under **La Liga's** soft salary cap, which limits what Spanish top-flight teams can spend on their playing and coaching staff each season, and would instead be continuing his career with …
**Paris Saint-Germain.**

# 34

# KNOW YOUR INFLUENCES: GEORGE WEAH (1966–)

The first African to be
European Player of the Year

GEORGE WEAH'S LIFE IS PROOF THAT FOOTBALL'S INFLUENCE CAN EXTEND WELL BEYOND THE PITCH AND INTO ALL SORTS OF UNLIKELY AREAS.

**That Weah ended up in football is surprising enough.** He grew up in one of the poorest areas of Liberia, an African country without a footballing tradition to boast of, and, before he was eventually picked up by **Monaco in France** at the age of 22, he had been working for the Liberian Telecommunications Corporation as a switchboard operator.

That all changed thanks to two men: **Claude Le Roy** and **Arsène Wenger**.

Le Roy was the **Cameroon national team coach** who discovered Weah. He contacted Wenger, then manager of **Monaco,** and, after a flight over to Liberia, **the future Arsenal manager signed the deal that put Weah on the European stage.**

**He was a phenomenal centre forward.** He moved from Monaco to Paris Saint-Germain, then on to AC Milan, where he would win Serie A twice and reach the summit of the sport. Weah was skilful, quick and graceful but also blessed with tremendous power. He was also one of the most natural finishers in the game and, unlike many of his attacking contemporaries in the **1990s,** was really more of an all-round forward than a penalty-area striker.

It made him unusual. It also made him a great influence on the next generation of star forwards, players like **Thierry Henry**, who were as regularly involved, and dangerous, outside the area as they were within it, and who would come to represent the future of centre-forward play.

Weah was that future before it happened. He won the **Ballon d'Or in 1995,** becoming the first African player to receive the award, and his talent and success challenged the false perception of African players, as being lacking in skill or finesse. There was no question that, at his peak, Weah was the world's best player.

He would also achieve another first. He entered politics after his retirement from football and was elected to his country's senate in 2014. Then, in 2018, he became the twenty-fifth president of Liberia.

# 35

# NO, THEY WON'T MAKE THE TRANSFER FEE BACK IN SHIRT SALES ALONE

## The economics of manufacturing deals explained

AFTER A BIG TRANSFER IS
COMPLETED AND A FAMOUS PLAYER IS SIGNED, HOW OFTEN HAVE YOU HEARD
SOMEONE SUGGEST THAT THE FEE IS IRRELEVANT, BECAUSE THE BUYING CLUB WILL
'MAKE THEIR MONEY BACK ON SHIRT SALES ALONE'.

## WELL, IT'S NOT TRUE. IT'S ONE OF THE GAME'S GREAT MYTHS, AND HERE'S WHY.

**Almost all clubs have manufacturing deals.** That's an agreement with a brand – Nike, Adidas, Umbro – that allows them to manufacture the club's playing kit, but also grants them the licence to sell replicas of it, too. These contracts are very, very lucrative: in 2016, for instance, **Chelsea** signed an agreement with **Nike** that guaranteed the club £60m each season for fifteen years.

And that's always the headline figure: what a brand is paying a club over the duration of the contract. **What it doesn't include, however, is the royalty split, which is always heavily in the manufacturer's favour – typically around 80–90%.**

THE MANUFACTURER

THE CLUB

THE DEAL

*UPFRONT PAYMENT – SPREAD OVER CONTRACTUAL YEARS*

*ROYALTY SPLIT IN MANUFACTURER'S FAVOUR (80–90%)*

That means that, while **signing famous players naturally causes shirt sales to spike, the club is not the main beneficiary when that happens**. In addition to which, many contracts include a clause that dictates that the team's share of the royalties only applies to sales above a certain volume.

Even if they didn't, though, if a club were only making 10% on the shirts they sold – priced individually at up to £100 each – then even selling a million shirts would only generate £10m in revenue, which is **nowhere close to covering even a medium-sized transfer fee for a top club**, let alone one required to buy a superstar of the game.

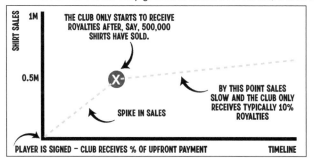

And the other problem is that people just don't buy that many football shirts – or at least not as many as everyone assumes.

In 2021, for instance, **Bayern Munich sold 3.25 million shirts worldwide**, more than any other club. **Real Madrid managed to sell just over 3 million** also and **Liverpool, ranked third, sold 2.45 million**. Healthy returns, of course, but nowhere near the figures expected. And what of Barcelona and Juventus, two extremely popular clubs who, at the time, were fielding Lionel Messi and Cristiano Ronaldo, the two most famous players in the world?

**Less than 3 million combined.**

For all the coverage it receives, football isn't quite the big business it's assumed to be. During the 2021–22 season, the twenty Premier League clubs combined announced collective annual revenue of around £5.3bn, which, although vast, hardly compares to the £65.7bn recorded by Procter & Gamble during the same period, or the £387.9bn of Amazon. In fact, the £5.3bn earned by twenty Premier League clubs only just exceeds the £4.8bn in revenue that Fortnite recorded in 2021.

**Football isn't as big as it seems.**

# 36

# SEE THE HIDDEN VALUE

**What football players
bring *off* the pitch**

WHEN REAL MADRID SIGNED DAVID BECKHAM FROM MANCHESTER UNITED IN 2003, IT WAS A TRANSFER THAT SHOOK THE WORLD. AT A TIME WHEN THE TRANSFER RECORD WAS JUST OVER £60M, FLORENTINO PÉREZ HAD SIGNED THE CROWN PRINCE OF ENGLISH FOOTBALL AND THE BIGGEST CELEBRITY THE SPORT HAD EVER KNOWN FOR A HEFTY, BUT NOT EXORBITANT, £25,000,000.

NOW, HE WASN'T GOING TO MAKE THAT BACK IN SHIRT SALES ALONE, BUT HE'D STILL GOT A BARGAIN.

CONTRACT
£25,000,000!

ESTADIO SANTIAGO BERNABEU

Truthfully, Pérez would have paid a lot more for Beckham if he'd had to – reportedly up to twice as much, which seems plausible given that he'd recently spent **£54m on Luis Figo, £60m on Zinedine Zidane and £40m on the original Ronaldo.**

**So why was Pérez prepared to pay through the nose** for an attacking talent when, for all intents and purposes, his side was already full of them?

Well, beyond being a world-class player, and famously serving as the face of traditional football manufacturers like **Adidas,** Beckham had fronted successful marketing campaigns for **Pepsi, Vodafone, Brylcreem and Marks & Spencer.** It proved his reach beyond football and outside sport as a whole. He had also been the first man to appear on the cover of the women's magazine **Marie Claire** and, in the summer of 2002, had driven **Japan and South Korea** into a frenzy at the World Cup. He appealed to people at home and abroad, and to men and women equally.

**That kind of visibility was particularly precious to Real Madrid.** All of its **Galácticos** (the name given to its highest-profile players) had it written into their contracts that the club was entitled to a 50% share of their **image rights,** which, for a player of Beckham's commercial viability, was extremely significant. It was part of the reason why Real's revenues roughly doubled between 2001 and 2005, and how a club that had been nearly €280m in debt at the turn of the century would find itself top of the **Deloitte Football Money League** just five years later.

But perhaps the extent to which Beckham's commercial value had been underestimated was shown soon after he arrived in Madrid. During his first 36 hours at the club, he was ferried between his ceremonial appointments in an **Audi,** as per an existing commercial agreement, and the exposure generated for the car manufacturer by the ensuing television coverage was, it is estimated, **substantial enough to repay a three-year investment in just three days.**

ljf find value

    file data script 48473838:
3385 file data script 59688488<
3734 file data script 459585478

    (44565 value generated)
    (04859 value generated)
    (03847 value generated)
    (67440 value generated)

    (47585 value generated)

# 37

# DIRECTORS OF FOOTBALL MATTER

### The value of club hierarchies

**IN THE OLD DAYS, FOOTBALL CLUBS USED TO CONSIST OF AN OWNER OR CHAIRMAN, WHO LOOKED AFTER THE BUSINESS, AND A MANAGER, WHO WAS IN CHARGE OF THE TEAM.**

**Today, with huge numbers of specialist employees on either side of that executive/technical divide, there's a need for someone to connect the two parts of the club – someone with credibility in both worlds.**

**That's a director of football;** or sporting director, technical director or general manager. Whatever the title, it's roughly the same role club to club, and, in real-world terms, it's the equivalent of a line manager for every football-specific member of staff employed by a football team.

That describes the size of the role. A director of football is usually a hidden figure, someone in a sharp suit who rarely does interviews with the media but who wields enormous power.

The average top-flight club is now a labyrinth of departments. Beyond the team itself and those immediately connected to it, there are **data departments, physios, youth teams, nutritionists and scouts.** The director of football is their boss; the person who all of those departments report to; who is ultimately responsible for hiring and firing; and who determines the club's sporting strategy. They are, in turn, accountable to the club's board and its owners.

What kind of players are being bought? What kind of youth player is the academy creating? Is the manager the right person to be coaching the first team? If not, who should replace them? **All of these decisions (and many, many others) involve different people, but ultimately rest with the director of football.**

For good reason, too. The old days were inefficient. Before directors of football became standard – over the last twenty years in England, in the decades before then everywhere else – a change in manager would nearly always involve a change in playing philosophy too, which in turn would necessitate a new set of players, a different recruiting focus and a turnover in staff. Needless to say, that came at tremendous hidden cost – a cost that is minimized if footballing appointments and decisions, like hiring coaches and signing players, are made by the same person over a long period of time.

It's not a guarantee of success, but the clarity and continuity of vision is what matters.

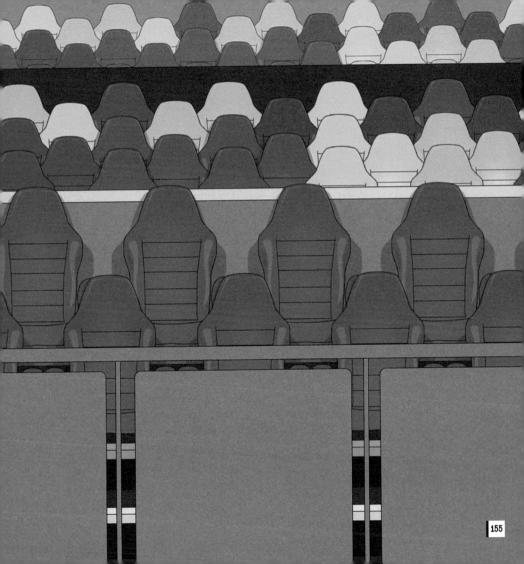

# 59%
## ACCURACY

# 7.8
## TACKLES + INTERCEPTIONS

# 5.2
## ASSISTS

# 6.3
## SUCCESSFUL PRESSURES

# 38

# SCOUTING MATTERS

How clubs decide on
the right players

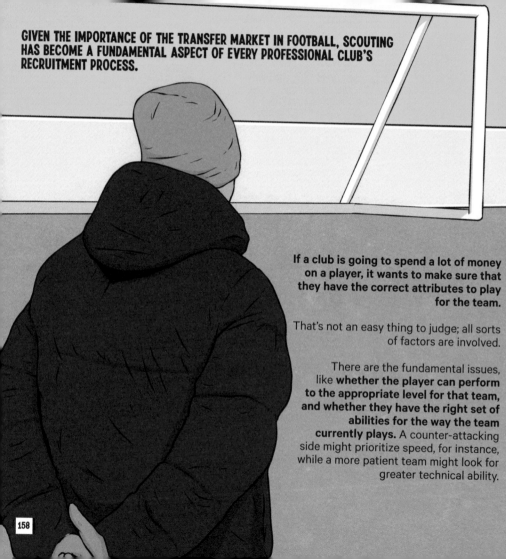

GIVEN THE IMPORTANCE OF THE TRANSFER MARKET IN FOOTBALL, SCOUTING HAS BECOME A FUNDAMENTAL ASPECT OF EVERY PROFESSIONAL CLUB'S RECRUITMENT PROCESS.

If a club is going to spend a lot of money on a player, it wants to make sure that they have the correct attributes to play for the team.

That's not an easy thing to judge; all sorts of factors are involved.

There are the fundamental issues, like **whether the player can perform to the appropriate level for that team, and whether they have the right set of abilities for the way the team currently plays.** A counter-attacking side might prioritize speed, for instance, while a more patient team might look for greater technical ability.

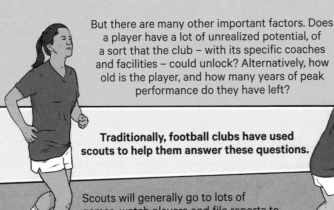

But there are many other important factors. Does a player have a lot of unrealized potential, of a sort that the club – with its specific coaches and facilities – could unlock? Alternatively, how old is the player, and how many years of peak performance do they have left?

**Traditionally, football clubs have used scouts to help them answer these questions.**

Scouts will generally go to lots of games, watch players and file reports to help their club build a picture of a player in case they want to sign them in the future. As part of their watching brief, they might also get to know family members and observe the player's personality and social habits. **For a lot of scouts, the person matters as much as the player.**

With the rise of technology, a new form of scouting has emerged, though. Many clubs now use **'data scouts' or 'video scouts'** to help them recruit. These scouts use more modern techniques such as data analysis or video scouting to help them assess players, often working in tandem with more traditional recruiting methods.

Using technology can allow clubs to cover a much broader pool of talent. Data analysis helps clubs to build more complete lists of players, while video scouting allows them to watch players from anywhere at the click of a button. It's a very large football world and, used correctly, a hybrid approach combining modern techniques with the more traditional 'eye-test' allows clubs to both save a great deal of time and focus on what they really need.

**39**

# YOU DON'T NEED TO GO FAR TO FIND VALUE

## The benefits of embracing home-grown talent

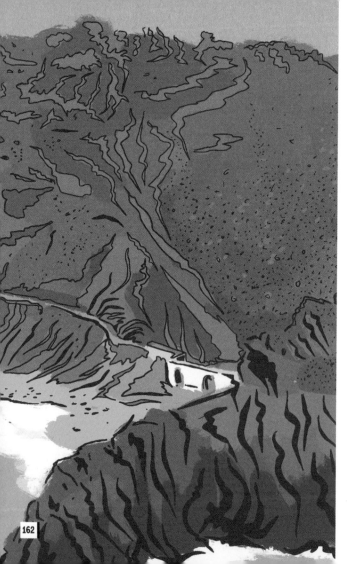

## THREE CLUB HAVE NEVER BEEN RELEGATED FROM SPAIN'S LA LIGA.

## BARCELONA, REAL MADRID AND ATHLETIC BILBAO.

**The first two aren't a surprise, but the team from Bilbao, the capital of the Basque Country, might well be.** Particularly because of their unique transfer policy. Or perhaps their longevity in Spain's top flight is because of it.

**Since 1911, Athletic Club have employed a Basque-only player policy**, meaning that only those born in the region, raised for a significant period within it, or whose parents were Basque may represent them. It's limiting, clearly, particularly within the context of modern cosmopolitan football, and yet **Athletic have never finished lower than fourteenth and have been Spanish champions eight times.**

So, given these self-imposed restrictions, how has this symbol of Basque separatism remained so successful?

Principally because of **Lezama,** the club's youth academy in Biscay. As of 2022, Athletic have spent over £10m on signing a player only four times in their history, and that reflects just how prolific a producer of talent they are.

According to a report by **CIES Football Academy** in May 2021, 40.6% of all first-team minutes in the 2020–21 season were played by homegrown players – **an enormously high figure.** During the same campaign, just 29.6% of Barcelona's first-team minutes went to **La Masia** products, and in England, **Brighton & Hove Albion** achieved the Premier League's highest rate of self-sufficiency, with 30.1% of their competitive minutes going to club-trained players.

## BUT WHY ARE ATHLETIC SO SUCCESSFUL AT DEVELOPING YOUNG PLAYERS?

In short, because they have to be. The academy and its production pathways are given much more emphasis than at most other clubs. It's supported by a network of around twenty full-time scouts and fed by 150 brother clubs in the region, which means that the coverage is so comprehensive as to be almost total. Athletic's prosperity hinges on never missing talent that emerges within their catchment area, and that vast network makes their nets very wide – unusually so, because most teams do not have such a range of supporting clubs and, as a result, are limited in their intake of young players.

It also because Athletic Club's Basque culture is so strong and that, by virtue of being regionally symbolic, they inspire a very rare form of local devotion from a young age. From a very early age, in fact.

## 'ANY BOY BORN WITHIN A 60KM RADIUS OF HERE IS SHOWERED WITH BALLOONS AND GIFTS,' FORMER PLAYER AND COACH JON SALOUN TOLD THE *GUARDIAN* IN 2018. 'MATERNITY WARDS ARE PLASTERED IN RED AND WHITE.'

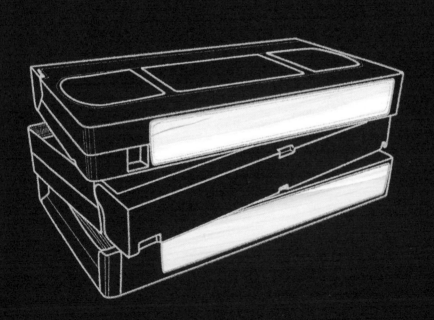

**40**

# KNOW YOUR INFLUENCES:
## MARCELO BIELSA
### (1955-)

Football's
uncompromising purist

MARCELO BIELSA, A SELF-CONFESSED FOOTBALL OBSESSIVE, IS FAMED FOR HIS RELENTLESS APPROACH TO PREPARATION AND WAS USING VIDEO TO SCOUT AND ANALYSE TEAMS WELL BEFORE IT BECAME WIDESPREAD.

His uncompromising approach inspires fierce loyalty in his players, many of whom have gone on to be successful coaches, including Mauricio Pochettino, Marcelo Gallardo and Diego Simeone, to name a few.

Bielsa is known for his intensive training, especially the famous **Murderball drill,** and extreme physical preparation is needed to play his fast vertical football with its emphasis on constant pressing. He has been tactically influential, creating the 3-3-1-3 formation and using midfielders as defenders to capitalize on their greater ball-playing ability. Bielsa likes his teams to create triangles of passing options to overload the opposition, and to baffle opposition marking systems with rotations among players. He also uses a spare player within a player-marking system – that is to say, nine outfield players tasked with player-marking duties, and one who isn't.

---

### TIFO EXPLAINS: MURDERBALL

Murderball became famous during Bielsa's time at Leeds. **The exercise is a normal 11 vs 11 game on a full-sized pitch, but with two key twists which are intended to ratchet the intensity to an extreme level.**

The **first** is that any time the ball goes out of play, another is immediately introduced, preventing any sort of stoppage in the game.

The **second** is that every participating player is assigned a stationary cone and, upon a new ball entering the pitch, all players must return to their cones before the game carries on.

---

Perhaps the most significant influence Bielsa has had was on **Pep Guardiola,** who visited him in **Mexico** in 2006. Over a barbecue, the two talked football for hours, and it was a transformational chat for the young Catalan. At the time, Guardiola was playing in Mexico and writing a tactics column for a Mexican newspaper, but he would soon return to Europe and go on to create some of the greatest club sides ever seen.

Bielsa has won an **Olympic gold medal** with **Argentina** in 2004 and Argentinian league titles with **Newell's Old Boys and Vélez Sársfield,** and most recently guided **Leeds** to an **EFL Championship** title in 2019–20.

# 41

# DON'T BE AFRAID OF xG

Football's expected goals
metric explained

EXPECTED GOALS, OR xG, IS ONE OF THE MORE COMPLICATED METRICS TO INVADE THE GENERAL AWARENESS OF FOOTBALL FANS. IT'S USED BY SOME CLUBS TO MEASURE PERFORMANCE AND BY RECRUITMENT TEAMS SEARCHING FOR VALUE, AND YOU EVEN SEE IT ON *MATCH OF THE DAY*.

What is it? Essentially, **xG is a means of understanding the quality of chances by estimating how likely it is that a shot will result in a goal, using a value from 0 to 1.** This calculation is based on a number of factors such as shot location, type of assisting pass, and, for some models, the location of the keeper and defenders. Expected Goals can be used for or against, so we can measure the quality of chances a team concedes, too.

**Clearly, it can be extremely useful.** Say there are two strikers, Alan and Anna. Alan has scored five non-penalty goals from an xG of 5.67 (we say 'non-penalty' because xG doesn't count penalties, whereas 'goals' does), while Anna has nine non-penalty goals from an xG of 4.23. Let's assume that they have both taken fifty shots and played ten games. Knowing all this means we can start to make conclusions about both strikers.

Because they've taken the same number of shots, Alan's higher xG total indicates his are better chances, perhaps because of location, or because they come from passes easier to control. And, although she's scored more, Anna's nine goals from an xG of 4.23 means she's converting these chances more often than we might expect, so there's a good chance her performance will drop off. Alan, on the other hand, has underperformed, which means he's likely to start scoring more.

## THIS IS WHERE xG CAN BE USEFUL.

In scouting, for example. With enough information, we can start to assess just how good these two players are. **On the surface, Anna's number of goals makes her seem like a better player than Alan. But looking at the xG, we can see that might not be the case.**

**xG also allows for valuable team assessment.**

Over a sensible period, probably a minimum of ten games, we can start to see whether teams are creating or giving up good chances relative to others. This means we can work out if they're overperforming or should improve over time compared to other teams in a league.

**42**

# HEAT DOESN'T EQUAL HOLIDAY

| Why mid-season tours
are important |

**Warm-weather training often infuriates fans** – the principle of it, at least. During a ten-day or two-week gap in the winter of a season that can sometimes extend to 60 games in nine months, teams don't just allow their players to rest at home. Instead, they jet off to Dubai or Saudi Arabia or Mallorca, often exposing their squads to the strain of long-haul flights and jet lag.

Added to which, these jaunts are enormously expensive, and the team's itinerary is always stuffed with lucrative friendlies, player appearances at local events and other commercial activities. Given that warm-weather training seems so disruptive, it's hardly surprising that it can provoke such a reaction.

## SO, WHY DO CLUBS DO IT?

Well, in the first instance, a different climate can quite literally offer more time. In January in the UK, a Premier League team might have around nine hours of daylight to work in. During the same month in Dubai, which has long been a popular destination, that's more like eleven; an obvious advantage.

Why can't they just play under floodlights? Because it's different. Sunshine makes for a contrasting playing experience to howling wind and driving, floodlit rain. A warmer climate means more pliable muscles. Less time spent warming up and – theoretically – less risk of injury or, at the very least, less time standing still in the cold receiving tactical instructions.

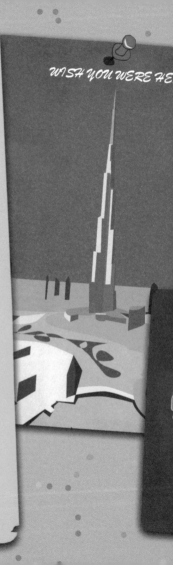

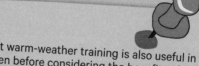

But warm-weather training is also useful in a subtle way. Even before considering the benefits of a mid-season change of environment and routine, there's the opportunity for a group of players to bond overseas and the emotional value in allowing them some time abroad. That might be particularly useful during a difficult season, if the trip allows players to briefly escape the scrutiny of disgruntled supporters or the grumbles of a critical media.

Either way, particularly for teams without state-of-the-art indoor facilities back home, the environment is more conducive to tuning the finer parts of the game, like positional play and shadow-play, or set-piece routines, and likely to inspire a better response from the players. **If it wasn't worth it, they wouldn't do it.**

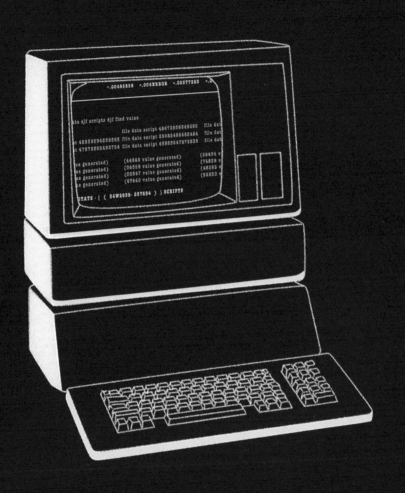

**43**

# KNOW YOUR INFLUENCES:
## VALERIY LOBANOVSKYI
## (1939–2002)

The innovator
behind the curtain

## PRESSING DIDN'T REALLY ORIGINATE IN GERMANY OR EVEN WITH TOTAL FOOTBALL IN THE NETHERLANDS.

Its origins can be traced back to **Ukraine** and **Viktor Maslov**, a Russian footballer who coached **Dynamo Kyiv** in the **1960s** and achieved great success with a form of 4-4-2 and an early style of pressing.

**His greatest protégé was Valeriy Lobanovskyi, a talented and flamboyant winger who won a league title and cup under him. Lobanovskyi, though, would reach greater heights as a coach.**

He won eight **Soviet Top League titles, six Soviet cups, and two Cup Winners' Cups** in an era when Soviet football was barely integrated into the rest of the European game. A trained engineer, Lobanovskyi was fascinated by cybernetics and statistics. He viewed each game as a system made of twenty-two elements (the players) divided into two subsets (the teams). Each subset was, he thought, greater than the sum of its parts – the skillset of individual players mattering less than the function of the team as a whole. He sought out ways for his teams to impose themselves on their opponents, viewing **football as a 'dialectic',** a struggle in which two forces constantly cause one another to alter. He drove his teams to change and adapt continuously on the pitch, dominating space and limiting their opponents' ability to take control of the game.

As Lobanovskyi said,

## 'IT IS NECESSARY TO FORCE THE OPPONENT INTO THE CONDITION YOU WANT THEM TO BE IN. ONE OF THE MOST IMPORTANT MEANS OF DOING THAT IS TO VARY THE SIZE OF THE PLAYING AREA.'

That meant stretching the play in attack and compressing it in defence, both very modern concepts that the Ukrainian explained perhaps better than anyone.

Added to this, Lobanovskyi was tactically experimental, sometimes playing without a recognized striker in the **1970s,** or using asymmetrical systems with lopsided wingers. He urged his full backs to attack, researched his opposition meticulously, and paid huge attention to set pieces. **In short, this was a very forward-thinking, systems-oriented coach, whose influence outside Russian and Ukrainian football is strikingly undervalued, but whose concepts and thinking proliferate throughout the modern game.**

179

## 44

# WHEN SOMETHING DOESN'T LOOK RIGHT, IT DOESN'T MEAN IT'S WRONG

The phenomenon of overlapping centre backs explained

**IN 2016, AS CHRIS WILDER AND ALAN KNILL SURVEYED THE MASSED RANKS OF DEFENDERS THWARTING THEIR SHEFFIELD UNITED SIDE IN THE ENGLISH LEAGUE ONE, THEY REALIZED AN INNOVATIVE SOLUTION WAS REQUIRED.**

**Winning football matches is about creating numerical advantages in different parts of the pitch, and getting players into dangerous areas to take advantage of space.** Wilder and Knill – manager and assistant – found a surprising way to do this and achieve promotion all the way to the Premier League: **overlapping centre backs.**

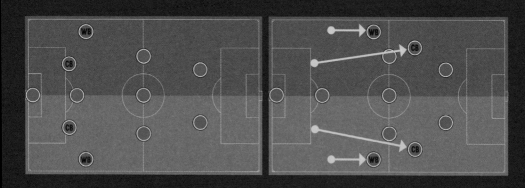

**Most centre backs stay fairly deep on the pitch in open play.** But, without a natural opposition marker, centre backs are also almost always free, except when pressed by a striker. This means they can pop up where least expected; it was this **element of surprise** that Wilder and Knill capitalized on.

And this is where the expression **'overlapping centre backs'** comes from. Sheffield United's centre backs often made the runs expected of their wing backs, pulling wider and pushing high up to deliver crosses, while the wing backs got forwards into more central, attacking positions. Opposition defenders, used to marking more orthodox systems, were baffled, and this meant United got players into dangerous areas, free of opposition.

The **Italian team Atalanta** under **Gian Piero Gasperini** are another good example: their centre backs pull very wide to offer passing options up the line and charge up field to deliver crosses, while also marking aggressively high up the pitch to stop opposition attacks.

It requires an unusual skill set from the players: they still need to be able to defend – to anticipate, tackle, mark and make clearances – but they must also possess more on-the-ball ability. It's risky, too, as they can be caught out of position and require cover from other players. **But when it works, with centre backs marauding up the pitch and runners slaloming infield, it can be devastating.**

## 45

# FOOTBALL IS ALWAYS EVOLVING

## The story of the no. 10 position

# A NO. 10 IS AN ATTACKING MIDFIELDER WHO TRIES TO FIND SPACE BETWEEN THE OPPOSITION DEFENSIVE AND MIDFIELD LINES, ORCHESTRATING ATTACKS AND LINKING THE STRIKERS TO THE REST OF THE SIDE.

**Tens are the team's guile, its craft, and perhaps the most revered of roles in many footballing cultures.** The greatest 10s in world football – **Lionel Messi, Marta, Diego Maradona** – have all epitomized the creativity and improvisation that gets fans out of their seats and wins games.

But, as football became increasingly physical, dominated by athletic teams of pressing players and strong defensive systems, **it felt as though the 10 was losing its place.** This is partly because luxury players – a term applied to **highly talented and creative players** with few defensive responsibilities – became obsolete, as everyone was required to pull their weight defensively.

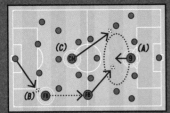

Creativity was also shared around more: **false 9s (A)**, **attacking full backs (B)**, and **deep-sitting passers (C)** could all be used to unlock sides, especially without the need to cover for another teammate. Added to which, **the 4-3-3 became extremely popular,** a formation without a natural home for an advanced playmaker.

**Nonetheless, the classic no. 10 position has made something of a comeback.**

**The rise of the 4-2-3-1,** a formation that does make room for the no. 10, has certainly helped. But these new 10s are also different and easier to accommodate. They're now more athletic and defensive and they're happy and willing to press without the ball. They no longer have a downside.

They also have different attacking traits. Some 10s are now more like a **second striker (D)**, and will make runs past a striker and towards goal, rather than – as was the case in the past - playing further away and creating chances for others.

And some central midfielders, who might have operated exclusively between the boxes in the past, can perform much of the function that 10s used to, but also play deeper when not in possession. These so-called **free 8s (E)** are close in creative essence to a 10, but far more versatile and with greater defensive responsibilities.

**THE NEW 10S ARE NOT THE SAME PLAYERS AS THE OLD 10S: THEY DON'T HAVE THE LANGUID GENIUS THAT USED TO CAPTURE THE IMAGINATION. BUT THEY DO HAVE MANY OF THE SAME ABILITIES, JUST PACKAGED IN A DIFFERENT WAY.**

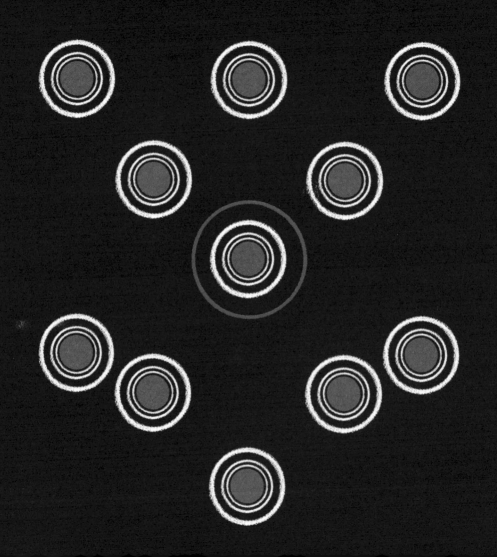

# 46

# KNOW YOUR INFLUENCES:
## CLAUDE MAKÉLÉLÉ
## (1973–)

The anchor man

IT'S NOT OFTEN THAT A FOOTBALLER GETS A POSITION NAMED AFTER THEM, BUT SUCH WAS CLAUDE MAKÉLÉLÉ'S INFLUENCE, PARTICULARLY ON THE PREMIER LEAGUE, THAT HE HAS SEALED HIS PLACE IN FOOTBALLING HISTORY.

The **'Makélélé role'** describes a **defensive midfielder who positions himself in front of the back four and patrols the space** with consummate awareness, anticipation, and no little steel, ultimately with the aim of providing a platform for more creative players.

Makélélé's ground-breaking role at the base of **Chelsea's** midfield three was developed under **José Mourinho,** and his function was to support two more attacking midfielders, while ensuring the team kept a solid base, and also covering forays by attacking full backs. His distribution was important, and Makélélé was certainly a far more technically proficient player than he's given credit for, but the 'defence first' connotations of the role are what it has come to mean.

**Now, though, the Makélélé role has evolved. It's extremely rare to see a defensive midfielder, or anchor man, who is merely that.** While the best teams benefit from a tough-tackling shield in front of the back line, especially with full backs taking such an attacking role, these players must also be able to pass to a high standard. The best, like **Rodri and Fabinho,** can spray the ball around like an attacking midfielder or carry it into dangerous areas. Their provision of defensive security is still critically important, but, as teams increasingly construct moves from the back, with short passes from the goalkeeper forward, the midfielder's ability to distribute and collect the ball from the centre backs, or even drop between them as a third passing option, is crucial.

Makélélé could probably have done this, too, but his arrival in the **Premier League** is associated with a tactical shift that over-emphasized defensive work. As Mourinho orchestrated the decline of a two-man midfield with his three, anchored by Makélélé, the defensive responsibilities of the spare player became dominant, and their attacking role overlooked. **Defensive midfielders are less focused on one function than they were before, but the player who gave the role its name was always more than that.**

# 47

# A LOT OF PEOPLE CARE ABOUT IT... AND ALWAYS HAVE

| The rise, fall and rise
of women's football |

**WOMEN'S FOOTBALL IS SURGING IN POPULARITY. BUT NOT FOR THE FIRST TIME.**

**IT ORIGINALLY EMERGED FROM THE MUNITIONS FACTORIES THAT SUPPLIED ARMS FOR THE FIRST WORLD WAR AND IT SPREAD LIKE WILDFIRE. MANY WOMEN HAD ENTERED THE WORKPLACE FOR THE FIRST TIME AND THEY SET UP TEAMS AND PLAYED MATCHES, THE TICKET SALES FROM WHICH RAISED MONEY FOR HOSPITALS AND FOR THE REHABILITATION OF WOUNDED SOLDIERS RETURNING FROM THE FRONT.**

By **1917,** there were enough teams to form a league, and in **May 1918, at the inaugural final of the Munitionettes' Cup, 22,000 people were in attendance at Ayresome Park in Middlesbrough.** It was amazing growth, but it wouldn't be allowed to continue.

In **1919,** government legislation forced women to leave their jobs in munitions factories, with the consequence that many football teams disbanded. Even so, many women continued to play and to help those who had returned wounded from the war, while also donating revenue from their ticket sales to workers – post-war Britain was rife with poverty and unemployment. This included supporting the **1921 Miners' strike**, a stance that had the effect of putting the women's game in direct opposition to the government.

Not that the players had many allies within their own sport. **In 1921, the FA Cup Final had attracted 50,000 fans.** A few months earlier, to the likely embarrassment of the Football Association, the enormously successful **Dick, Kerr Ladies** had played an exhibition match at Goodison Park that attracted over **53,000 supporters.**

The atmosphere was quickly changing. It also didn't help that the game's pioneering players were icons of female empowerment, flouting social conventions at a time when women were being encouraged to return to their traditional place at home. A previously supportive press had begun publishing contrived medical advice from leading doctors, in which it was claimed that women's bodies were unsuitable for football.

Then, in **December 1921,** the FA – citing that advice and also making vague and unsubstantiated comments about the misappropriation of gate receipts – **banned its member clubs from allowing women's matches on their grounds,** starving the players of facilities and curtailing the game's growth.

## IT WAS A DEVASTATING BLOW. REMARKABLY, IT WOULD TAKE ANOTHER FIFTY YEARS AND A UEFA INTERVENTION FOR THE BAN TO BE LIFTED.

**48**

# KNOW YOUR INFLUENCES: MARTA
## (1986–)

The human
highlight reel

**'MARTA IS THE BIGGEST NAME IN WOMEN'S FOOTBALL. SHE WON SO WE COULD GET TO THE LEVEL WE ARE TODAY. EVERYTHING WE HAVE ACHIEVED IN THE GAME CAME THROUGH HER, EVEN IF WOMEN'S FOOTBALL EXISTED BEFORE.'**

This is how **Thais Monteiro,** an attacking midfielder for **Grota de Niterói,** described the impact of the **Brazilian Marta Vieira da Silva** on the women's game. And she isn't wrong. Marta was one of the first icons of the women's game in the modern period.

Ask most people to name things that they associate with Marta and more often than not you're likely to hear the answer **'Brazil'.** Marta debuted for the country's national team, or **Seleção,** back in 2002 at the age of 16 and hasn't looked back since. She has played 171 times for her country, picking up 115 goals in the process: enough to make her the highest scorer across both the men's and the women's game.

**During the 2019 World Cup, she also became the first player – male or female – to score at five World Cup tournaments and her seventeen goals across the course of those five World Cup tournaments are also unmatched.**

So, she has an incredible legacy, but Marta has also been an entertainer. A player of wonderful skill and a magical left foot, her goals have often been little works of art. Her close control and dribbling ability frequently baffled opponents, and she scored goals of rare watchability with both feet, from close range and distance, and at a time when cut-through for women's football was rare and precious and important.

**She's a Brazilian great who transcended the gender divide and who deserves her place alongside Pelé, Ronaldo and Ronaldinho, and who has contributed enormously to the great health in which women's football finds itself today.**

# 49

# KEEP AN EYE OUT FOR SPORTSWASHING

## How football is being used for influence

INCREASINGLY, GOVERNMENTS AND OLIGARCHS AROUND THE WORLD ARE TURNING TO SPORT AS A MEANS OF EXERCISING SOFT POWER — OF GAINING POLITICAL AND CULTURAL INFLUENCE OR PRESTIGE THROUGH SELF-PROMOTION, RATHER THAN FORCE, THREATS OR SANCTIONS. FOOTBALL, AS THE MOST SUCCESSFUL AND IMPORTANT GLOBAL SPORT, IS VIEWED AS A PARTICULARLY EFFECTIVE AVENUE FOR THIS.

**Soft power** can be flexed through the sponsorship of major sporting events – think of **the Russian state-owned Gazprom's sponsorship of the UEFA Champions League –** or through the hosting of major tournaments, like the **Qatar 2022 World Cup,** which will hope to present a country with a dismal human rights record in a new, more favourable light.

2022 is the culmination of a much longer soft-power campaign by the Qatari government, which has established a football school, **Aspire Academy,** which now has links to clubs in **England, Belgium and Spain** and which has hosted around 500 international sports events since 2005, from handball to boxing to gymnastics, while also hosting football matches such as the **Turkish Super Cup and two World Club Cups.**

**All the while, during the twelve years since the tournament was awarded, 6,500 migrant workers are reported to have died in Qatar.**

**It's a calculated risk.** Do the reputational benefits of staging a tournament outweigh the cost and criticism that come with such international exposure? During the qualification stages for the **World Cup,** several teams, including the **German and Norwegian national sides,** wore protest T-shirts before games, directing the public's attention towards – among other issues – the human rights abuses occurring in the region.

But critical scrutiny is an easier exercise when its focus is many thousands of miles away.

Over the past two decades, European football has seen an influx of new investors, many of whom have been able to use the game to engineer changes in perception, either of themselves or of their region.

**Oligarchs of all stripes** have become stakeholders in European football, as have **sovereign wealth funds from Qatar, Saudi Arabia and Abu Dhabi.**

Each time, the routine is the same: the club in question is lavished with new wealth, better players and a line of famous coaches, and the local catchment area might even be regenerated at great expense.

But the aim is always more than just to show benevolence: many investors hope that sporting success interests the world more than whatever reputation they might be attempting to improve, repair or launder.

**50**

# COUNT TO 50...THEN ADD ONE

### Fan ownership and the 50+1 rule explained

# GERMAN FOOTBALL IS OFTEN REVERED OUTSIDE GERMANY.

It's loud and colourful, people can drink beer in the stands, and the fan experience is much more welcoming and – generally – reflective of the region. As ticket prices have soared across the continent, particularly in England, they've remained affordable for German fans. And when the biggest clubs in Europe attempted a coup in January 2021, proposing the formation of a new Super League, **German clubs were among those who refused to join.**

# PART OF THE REASON FOR ALL OF THIS IS THE 50+1 RULE.

**Before 1998, German football clubs were owned by their members and run on a not-for-profit basis.** Their football teams were part of multi-sport organizations and, crucially, had no avenue for any external investment or outside takeover. There were also fewer funds for transfers and team-building.

**By the 1990s,** the commercial age had begun across Europe. The game's popularity was growing, revenues from decadent new broadcasting contracts were flowing into the game, and new, state of the art, all-seater stadiums were being built, attracting a wealthier, more middle-class fan. Owning a football club, which had previously been a labour of vanity and ego, was beginning to become prestigious, and a way of not just making money but also exerting influence. The types of people interested in acquiring the clubs, particularly in England, were starting to change.

**In Germany, that left teams facing a significant disadvantage.** Without the opportunity for investment, teams ran the risk of being left behind and finding themselves unable to compete within the developing market-place.

The solution was a compromise between the past and the future. **From 1998 onwards,** clubs were allowed to essentially outsource their football divisions, turning them into separate entities. But there was one important restriction: **the members-run sports club had to retain a 50% holding in the new organization, plus one share – meaning that it would have to retain majority control.**

# HENCE THE EXPRESSION: 50+1.

**There are exceptions.** If – for instance – a company or individual had provided significant support to a club over twenty years or more prior to 1998, they were exempt from 50+1. That applies to **Volkswagen's** relationship with **Wolfsburg,** for instance, and the **Bayer pharmaceutical company's patronage of Bayer Leverkusen.**

Whatever the fine detail, the intention of 50+1 is clear. It gives clubs the opportunity to run themselves on a commercial basis and to attract investment from the outside, but it also offers a theoretical safeguard against undesirable ownership or business practices and the myriad issues that are associated with those problems. **It would be very difficult, for instance, for a German club to ever be used for sportswashing.** Nor could a team, in theory, become reliant on a single, individual source of wealth, or have its identity changed against its fans' will. **50+1 ensures that the German football fan is a supporter, rather than a customer.**

# 51

# KNOW YOUR INFLUENCES:
## AMR FAHMY
## (1983-2020)

The hero you
hadn't heard of

## YOU OFTEN READ ABOUT HEROES ON THE PITCH, BUT AMR FAHMY WAS A HERO ON THE TERRACES.

Amr was born in Cairo in Egypt and became a huge fan of Africa's biggest club side, Al Ahly. But watching wasn't enough. After studying in Milan and experiencing the fire and the fury of the Italian ultra movement – organized fans who dedicate their lives to following their teams with banners and flares – he decided in 2007 to set up Egypt's first ultra group.

The Ahlawy started as a few hundred friends but mushroomed to tens of thousands from a cross section of Cairo society – rich and poor, male and female, devout and secular, Muslim and Christian – all singing songs and flying banners about the privations of living under a dictatorship. **In 2011 the Arab Spring swept the region and the ultras played an important role in toppling the country's dictator Hosni Mubarak.** The Ahlawy, once seen as hooligans, now saw their songs become the soundtrack of the revolution.

**Then tragedy struck. Seventy-two Al Ahly fans were killed by violent thugs at a match against Al Masry in Port Said.** Amr and the Ahlawy organized a year-long boycott of the league until justice was served. An Egyptian court later found there had been collusion between **Egyptian security figures and the ultras of Al Masry** to attack the Al Ahly fans.

Eventually the revolution ended with a military coup and the ultras were outlawed, considered terrorists. Many were jailed. **The Ahlawy burned their banner and disbanded.** Amr's true identity as a revolutionary capo was kept secret, as his father was general secretary of the **Confederation of African Football.** Incredibly, Amr followed in his father's footsteps and brought the ultra's black and white morality to CAF.

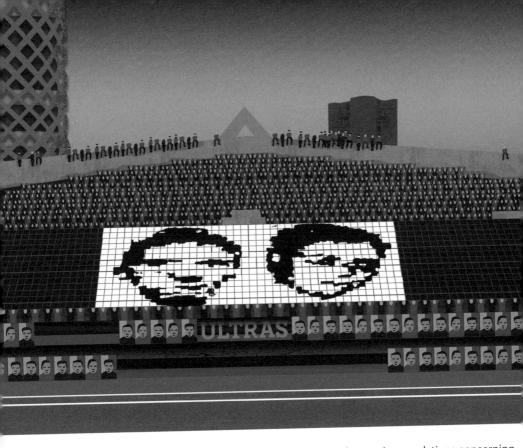

He exposed corruption, and was sacked in April 2019 for his embarrassing revelations concerning the conduct of CAF president Ahmad Ahmad. CAF wouldn't get away with it that easily. He decided to run for president himself. **His revelations helped to bring down Ahmad Ahmad, who was barred by FIFA from standing for re-election.** But Amr never saw it. In February 2020 he died of brain cancer. He was 37 years old.

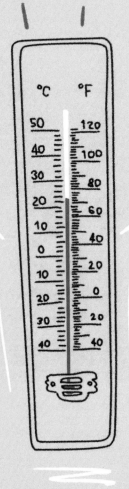

# 52

# PREPARE FOR THE FUTURE

## The impact of the climate crisis on football

## THERE ARE CURRENTLY NINETY-TWO LEAGUE TEAMS IN ENGLAND. BY 2050, TWENTY-THREE OF THEM CAN EXPECT PARTIAL OR TOTAL ANNUAL FLOODING OF THEIR STADIUMS.

**That's an alarming projection, but one football needs to respond to, with rising sea levels being just one consequence of global climate change.** In fact, extreme weather has already begun to regularly affect sporting events. In 2019, for instance, **the Rugby World Cup in Japan** was plunged into chaos by unprecedented Pacific typhoons, and earlier that year **the Australian Open in Melbourne** was heavily disrupted by smoke blowing in from the country's devastating bushfires.

When **the 2020 Tokyo Olympics** was eventually staged, a year later than planned, it would prove the warmest in history, with events having to be moved to cooler parts of the day and several athletes fainting in the heat. Mike Tipton, a Professor in Human and Applied Physiology at the University of Portsmouth, suggested that the Olympics might have to move to the autumn in future to combat the effects of climate change.

Of course, many of football's showpiece events already occur during the summer and, while governing bodies have introduced cooling breaks to tournament matches, treatment for spectators suffering from heat exhaustion will probably become commonplace too, as will measures to keep in-stadium temperatures safe.

But this isn't just a summer problem. Of those twenty-three British stadiums exposed to flooding by 2050, the Cardiff City and KCOM Stadiums will both **be entirely underwater,** Grimsby's Blundell Park will be in the North Sea, while the Riverside Stadium in Middlesbrough **will only be accessible by boat.** In the Premier League, Chelsea's Stamford Bridge and West Ham's London Stadium will **experience flooding on an annual basis,** as will Southampton's St Mary's.

In Germany, **Werder Bremen's Weserstadion** will also partially flood annually by 2050, while **Bordeaux's Matmut Atlantique** will flood completely. In the Netherlands, **ADO Den Haag, Heerenveen and Groningen** will all experience total flooding every twelve months, too.

**And football is a contributor to climate change, not just a victim of it.** According to a 2019 study, the game has an output of roughly 10,000,000 tonnes of carbon each year. For context, that's equivalent to the annual output of Bolivia.

1. KEEPMOAT STADIUM

2. BLUNDELL PARK

3. RIVERSIDE STADIUM

4. KCOM STADIUM

NORTH SEA

UK

IRELAND

ENGLISH CH

5. CARDIFF CITY STADIUM

6. ST MARY'S STADIUM

7. STAMFORD BRIDGE

8. LONDON STADIUM

9. CARROW ROAD

THE NINETY-TWO PROFESSIONAL TEAMS IN THE TOP FOUR LEAGUES IN THE 2019–20 SEASON. NUMBERED ARE SOME OF THE TWENTY-THREE CLUBS THAT CAN EXPECT PARTIAL OR TOTAL ANNUAL FLOODING OF THEIR STADIUMS BY 2050.

215

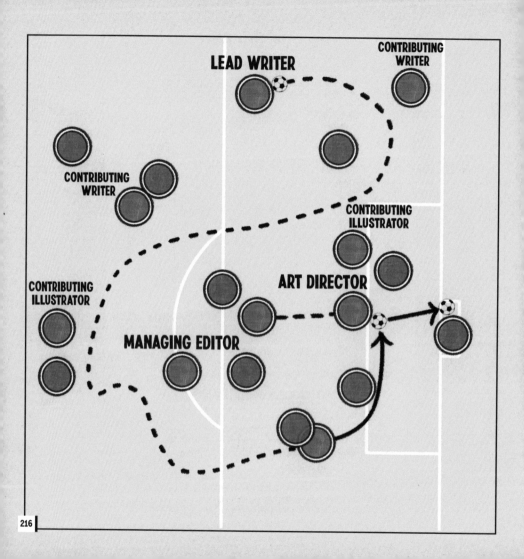

# MEET THE TIFO TEAM

## ALICE DEVINE

ART DIRECTOR

## SEB STAFFORD-BLOOR

LEAD WRITER

## JOE DEVINE

MANAGING EDITOR

## OTHER CONTRIBUTORS

Philippe Fenner
Henry Cooke
Marco Bevilacqua
Craig Silcock

Alex Stewart
Jon Mackenzie
JJ Bull

PENGUIN BOOKS

UK | USA | Canada | Ireland | Australia
India | New Zealand | South Africa

Penguin Books is part of the Penguin Random House group of companies
whose addresses can be found at global.penguinrandomhouse.com

First published 2022
002

Printed and Bound in Latvia by Livonia Print

The authorized representative in the EEA is Penguin Random House Ireland,
Morrison Chambers, 32 Nassau Street, Dublin D02 YH68

A CIP catalogue record for this book is available from the British Library

ISBN: 978–0–241–60937–8

www.greenpenguin.co.uk

MIX
Paper from
responsible sources
FSC® C018179

Penguin Random House is committed to a
sustainable future for our business, our readers
and our planet. This book is made from Forest
Stewardship Council® certified paper.